VOICES OF STUDENT TEACHERS
Cases from the Field

Second Edition

Muriel K. Rand
Jersey City State College

Sharon Shelton-Colangelo
Northwest Vista College

Merrill
Prentice Hall

Upper Saddle River, New Jersey
Columbus, Ohio

Library of Congress Cataloging in Publication Data

Vice President and Publisher: Jeffery W. Johnston
Executive Editor: Debra A. Stollenwerk
Assistant Editor: Daniel J. Parker
Production Editor: Kimberly J. Lundy
Production Coordination: Clarinda Publication Services
Design Coordinator: Diane C. Lorenzo
Photo Coordinator: Kathleen Kirtland
Cover Designer: Super Stock
Cover Image: Thomas Borah
Production Manager: Pamela D. Bennett
Director of Marketing: Ann Castel Davis
Marketing Manager: Krista Groshong
Marketing Coordinator: Tyra Cooper

This book was set in Christiana by The Clarinda Company, and was printed and bound by R. R. Donnelley & Sons Company. The cover was printed by The Lehigh Press, Inc.

Photo Credits: pp. 1, 93, 163: Anthony Magnacca/Merrill; pp. 9, 37, 65: Scott Cunningham/Merrill; p. 10: KS Studios/Merrill; p. 112: Tom Watson/Merrill; p. 138: Anne Vega/Merrill.

Pearson Education Ltd.,
Pearson Education Australia Pty. Limited
Pearson Education Singapore Pte. Ltd
Pearson Education North Asia Ltd.
Pearson Education Canada, Ltd.
Pearson Educación de Mexico, S.A. de C.V.
Pearson Education—Japan
Pearson Education Malaysia Pte. Ltd.
Pearson Education, *Upper Saddle River, New Jersey*

Merrill
Prentice Hall

10 9 8 7 6 5 4 3 2 1
ISBN 0-13-094130-1

Preface

How do we develop student teachers who are reflective practitioners? Most teacher preparation programs recognize the importance of reflection and of creating experiences that help students reflect on their teaching experiences. This text provides a venue for students to step outside their practice and bridge the gap between the educational theory presented in college courses and the complex realities of today's classrooms. Student teachers occupy a unique position: although they are not yet real teachers, they also are no longer fully students; indeed, they shoulder a full array of responsibilities in the classroom. Caught in the middle of demands from their own students, their cooperating teachers, their college supervisors, and their education professors, these novice teachers often struggle to reconcile a host of particular issues and dilemmas. Student teachers need support to make sense of this busy, complicated, exhausting, but important period in their professional lives. This text, containing real-life teaching cases of student teachers' experiences, provides a way for them to reflect, reconsider, and rethink the events they experience.

New to This Edition

In this revised edition, new cases have been added covering current issues such as using the Internet in teaching, standards-based teaching and assessment, and the effect of traumatic events in students' lives. Discussion questions after each case and a chart on the inside covers that summarizes the issues covered in each case help instructors link the cases to topics covered in class. Many of the cases are set in urban schools and there is extended coverage of middle school and high school cases, but they still are generalized across all grades and settings. The sections of the book have been reorganized, with new sections added on *Challenges of Ethical Dilemmas* and *Challenges of Working with Families*. In each section, cases are ordered by grade level so that locating specific age groups is easier. An updated, annotated bibliography provides suggestions for further reading to encourage students to explore issues more deeply and to develop the habit of finding resources to improve their teaching.

The cases lend themselves to many topics and are best used in conjunction with other readings, experiences, and related activities. Since by their nature these cases focus on problems, it is important to provide readers with a balanced perspective on teaching. This book will be useful in seminar courses taken in conjunction with student teaching or in courses with earlier practicum experiences. These cases will also stimulate discussion and raise issues for introductory educational foundations courses and illustrate principles covered in educational psychology and philosophy.

Case-Based Pedagogy

Teaching cases have established themselves as an important pedagogical tool in teacher education. Cases offer the opportunity for students to construct their own understanding, work at their own level, have choice in the curriculum, and, most of all, be active participants in their own learning. Cases are an ideal bridge between theory and practice and support a constructivist view of learning.

The real-life cases in *Voices of Student Teachers: Cases from the Field* reveal the unique problems and issues that student teachers face. These cases describe actual dilemmas students confronted during their internships and are an ideal mechanism to enable beginning teachers to analyze and reflect on their own practice. The cases provide a repertoire of experiences from which students can draw to meet new challenges and explore possibilities in their own teaching. Discussing these dilemmas duplicates the process of professional growth described by Donald Schön, who explains, "A professional practitioner is a specialist who encounters certain types of situations again and again. . . . As a practitioner experiences many variations of a small number of types of cases, he is able to 'practice' his practice. He develops a repertoire of expectations, images, and techniques. He learns what to look for and how to respond to what he finds" (1987, p. 60).

Peer Collaboration in Case Analysis

The value of these cases for reflection lies in the potential for sharing different perspectives during peer discussions. By analyzing cases in the college classroom, students will be able to think differently about the problems they encounter during their student teaching and beyond. These cases give prospective teachers an opportunity to think about the many possible ways in which a problem can be addressed. Ideally student teachers will also develop a habit of reflection: regularly thinking about what could be improved or what else would have worked in any given situation. When student teachers work with their peers to analyze and discuss cases, they are better able to function within their zone of proximal development (Vygotsky, 1978) and to collaboratively construct meaning. In working with peers on cases, student teachers can be more resourceful, more thoughtful, and generally more competent than they could be on their own. The group discussions and reflections scaffold the students' growth and move them forward in their professional development.

Organization of This Book

The general framework we used in organizing this book parallels the way in which we use cases in our teaching:

- *Introducing students to cases.* In Part I we show students how to read and analyze cases and what can be learned from teaching cases. This section also demonstrates how to work together as a group, use active listening, and brainstorm ideas. We encourage students to think about the process of decision making in their teaching and to put themselves in the place of the student teacher in the case.

- *Presenting teaching cases.* Part II gives students practice in analyzing cases that cover a wide range of issues. The cases in Sections 1 through 6 are grouped according to major topics of Creating Classroom Communities, Curriculum and Instruction, Diversity, Working with Families, Ethical Dilemmas, and Working with Other Professionals. Although the cases are ordered by grade level within each section, we encourage you to choose individual cases that fit your needs and use them in the order that makes sense for your teaching. To help you select appropriate cases, we begin each one with a short abstract that gives pertinent details about the case.

- *Writing your own teaching case.* After analyzing various cases in our classes, our students write their own cases as a formalized way of reflecting on their teaching. Part III presents guidelines for prospective teachers to follow in writing their own cases and explains the value of using writing as a form of reflection.

How These Cases Were Developed

The cases in this collection are authentic narratives collected from student teachers studying at an urban university in New Jersey. The majority of these students are from working-class families in which they are the first generation to attend college. About half the authors are nontraditional students: mothers returning to college, older men changing careers, people in their late 20s who spent time in business and now would like to teach, and so on. Many of them are African-American or Latino, and about half speak English as a second language or are bilingual. Many of the students were raised in an urban environment and attended urban public schools or urban Catholic schools.

These cases reflect the realities of classrooms. The advantage of written cases, as opposed to videotaped teaching episodes, is that they provide both the observable actions that happen in the classroom and the thoughts, reactions, and background information of the student teachers as the story unfolds. The students were not simply reporting events but rather were interpreting them through their own eyes and constructing their own meaning of the events. We believe that the cases are open enough for readers to be able to put themselves into the student teachers' places. No resolutions are provided; each case ends with a problem, challenge, or dilemma facing the student teacher. Most narratives are relatively short, with enough details to encourage discussion but without extensive reflection from the writer. This allows learners who are reading the cases to mentally re-create the situation and rethink the possible actions through their own reflection.

We hope that this book provides fertile ground for preparing new teachers and that our readers continue their lifelong professional growth through reflection, questioning, and sharing their own stories.

For Further Reading

Schön, D. (1987). *Educating the reflective practitioner.* San Francisco: Jossey-Bass.
Vygotsky, L. S. (1978). *Mind in society: The development of higher psychological processes.* Cambridge, MA: Harvard University Press.

Acknowledgments

We are indebted to the following reviewers, who shared their insights and added clarity to the book: Sandra L. DiGiaimo, University of Scranton; Karen Kusiak, Colby College; Sarah Moore, University of Kentucky; Mike Perl, Kansas State University; Elizabeth Simons, Alexandria City Public Schools, Virginia; and Barbara Stanley, Valdosta State University.

Contributors

Many thanks to the authors who contributed cases to this book:

Valerie Aguanno	Marni Greenberg	Nancy Moreno
Idalia Alvarez	Pat Griffith	Lisa Nisbet
Anthony Ammirata	William Hanson	Liliana Ortiz
Leo Boice	Kelleen Haughney	Jim Pedersen
Janine Bucco	Howard Helman	Laura Perez
Marianne Calabrese	Brandi Herring	Julio Piña
Luz Castillo	Miguel Jimenez	Tammy Poggi
Debbie Cherreun	L. Diane Jones	Kerri Lee Ranaudo
Harriet Nadja Clark	Robert Keating	Giovanna Ricciardone
Patrick R. Cullen, Jr.	Christine Loennecker	Margaret Rothberg
Constance A. DeJoseph	Michele Danielle Maggio	Victoria Russo
Arlene Diaz	Michelle Manzo	Marlene Sueiro
Cheryl DiFilippis	Serena Marra	Sheila Tapley
Lillian Esquivel	Carrie Mazak	Paul Tavarone
Melissa Fink	Kim McAvoy	Patricia Taylor
Kim Geddes	Heather McClary	Janet Thomas
Tanya Gilliam	Laura McKeon	Peter Verga
		Cara Zebrowski

Thanks also to the many, many students whose cases could not be included because of space limitations. Like most teachers, we have learned more than our students as we continue together on the journey toward improving our teaching.

Brief Contents

Contents

student who is new to the district, James, is making it difficult for her to develop her skills as a teacher. While her cooperating teacher agrees that James needs to be evaluated, Melinda still must cope with his disruptive activities until the best placement for him can be determined.

Section 3   Challenges of Diversity   65

Section 5   Challenges of Ethical Dilemmas   112

Section 6   Challenges of Working with Other Professionals 138

are detracting from her student teaching in a high school where she hopes to be hired.

Part III   *Reflecting on Teaching: Writing Your Own Case   163*

PART I
To the Student

If this is your first experience with teaching cases, you may be wondering what exactly a case is, how to work with cases, and what you can learn from them. The cases in this book are all told by student teachers and are about actual problems, challenges, or issues that they faced. We chose these particular stories because we felt that each is a good example of a common or significant issue for student teachers. Being a student teacher is different from being a full-fledged practicing teacher in your own classroom, and these cases reflect that unique and demanding position.

The cases in this book are dilemma-based. We know such cases can be frustrating to read because they have no resolution. Nevertheless, we leave you hanging on purpose, allowing you to brainstorm and analyze what the student teacher might do. It is important to remember that there is no one right answer, just as there is no one right path to follow in teaching.

We are somewhat hesitant about offering a book that focuses just on the problems of teaching and learning, and we hope the book will not discourage you.

Remember that these cases were collected from hundreds of students who also had many joyful, successful learning experiences during their student teaching.

Why Use Cases?

Teaching cases stimulate your thinking about the many possible actions that can be taken in any given situation in the classroom. When you are in the classroom making spur-of-the-moment decisions, it is difficult to stop, reflect on, and analyze each one. Reading about the dilemmas in these cases allows you to step back, stop the action, and think about all the factors that influence each decision. You are freed from the actual consequences of the action, so you can mentally experiment with a variety of possibilities.

When it comes to analyzing cases, two heads really are better than one, and a small group may be the best learning situation of all. We hope these cases will generate rich discussions with your peers, providing new ideas and ways of clarifying your own thinking. Everyone who reads a case brings his or her unique cultural experiences, philosophy, and personal understanding to the case discussion. As you work together to coordinate the different perspectives of the group members, you may be surprised by ideas you never thought of, frustrated by outlooks you disagree with, and relieved that other students face challenges similar to your own.

Studying cases also helps you build a repertoire of experiences, even though they may not have been firsthand. This is akin to a virtual reality classroom in which you can "practice" being a teacher. We believe that later, when you are teaching in your own classroom and similar situations arise, you will already have begun to think about the issues involved and be able to make better decisions.

Most important, we believe that analyzing and discussing cases will help you develop the habit of reflecting on your practice. This involves stepping back and looking at the challenges of teaching from many different perspectives. Then you can decide what possible actions can be taken, what results can be expected, and what other factors may be affecting the situation. You will learn "reflection in action" (as Donald Schön describes the process) and have the potential to devise new methods of reasoning, new categories of understanding, new strategies of action, and new ways of framing problems (Schön, 1987, p. 39).

As part of this process of reflecting on your own teaching, we encourage you to write your own teaching case to share with your peers. Part III of this book helps you through this process, giving you guidelines and ideas for using writing as a way of improving your teaching. Writing cases also gives you the opportunity to share your own experiences with others and get their feedback.

How to Read a Case

First, read straight through a case, putting yourself in the student teacher's place. Try to experience the case as if it were happening to you. Next, go back and write down your personal response to the case. Reread sections as necessary to get the details straight in your mind. Since the information in cases is somewhat limited, you may find that information you wish to know is missing. Then try to determine which factors need to be considered in deciding what to do next. Gradually you will come to some conclusion about what you would do if you were in the student teacher's place. Once again, remember that there is never one right answer, no one solution that is implied. Real teaching, like these cases, is complex and messy and cannot be done well with one standard approach.

Discussing Teaching Cases

Two strategies that can help groups analyze and discuss cases more deeply and effectively are active listening and brainstorming.

Active Listening

Active listening is a simple but powerful strategy that involves carefully listening to the speaker, reflecting back his or her ideas, and actively assisting in developing the speaker's thinking. Too often in our society, we communicate through a sort of argumentative defensiveness, each speaker contrasting his or her views with those of another. Occasionally, someone who is empathic will break through this conversational pattern with a comment such as "I know what you mean," though even here the listener may be tempted to shift the discussion to something he or she has experienced. As a result, neither person may have really heard the other but has used the discussion to air his or her own views. Under these circumstances little learning takes place.

By contrast, careful listening can contribute to the learning of everyone involved in a conversation, listeners and speakers alike. Not only can listeners come into contact with ideas they may never have considered previously, but speakers can feel validated when they are heard and thereby more able to productively consider feedback. When you are discussing a case, listening can foster a sense of community that can deepen the reflective capabilities of all concerned.

To see the difference between ordinary conversation and active listening, choose four volunteers to enact the following dialogues. As you read along, notice which comments seem to help the student articulate his thinking and make a decision about what to do and which comments are unhelpful.

Dialogue 1

Joel: I have a problem turning in tomorrow's homework.
Ms. Grant: Well, it's due then, and you'll either turn it in or get a zero.
Joel: But tonight is the big game, and Coach says we have to suit up right after dinner.
Ms. Grant: You should have planned ahead. You knew about this game all week.
Joel: I've been busy all week.

MS. GRANT: Look, I'd like to help you, but if I made an exception in your case, I'd have to make it for everyone.

JOEL: Oh, all right. Just give me the zero.

DIALOGUE 2

JOEL: I have a problem turning in tomorrow's homework.

MS. GRANT: What problem are you having?

JOEL: Tonight is the big game, and Coach says we have to suit up right after dinner.

MS. GRANT: Being so involved on the team must cause a lot of conflicts for you.

JOEL: Yeah, especially for this last week!

MS. GRANT: It sounds like you've had to work hard to turn in your homework during the last week.

JOEL: I've been so busy that I haven't even called Amy.

MS. GRANT: So you're worried that you haven't called her?

JOEL: Well, actually, it's part of the problem I'm facing today. We had practice all last week, and I was so busy that I couldn't call Amy. I'm afraid she's mad at me.

MS. GRANT: How is that part of your problem today?

JOEL: I was thinking of calling her after school.

MS. GRANT: So I gather what you are saying is that you don't know whether to do your homework after school or call Amy.

JOEL: Yeah! That's right. Maybe I could just do the homework this afternoon before dinner and then explain to Amy how busy I've been when I see her at the game. Thanks, Ms. Grant. I always feel better when I talk over my problems with you.

You can see from these dialogues how easily we can open or close communication by the responses we give as listeners. To open up and share ideas, you and your classmates must all feel psychologically safe from judgment and evaluation. Nothing shuts down participation as quickly as negative comments. With active listening, you acknowledge the speaker's words by restating them to show you've understood without giving advice or being judgmental. This helps any misunderstandings come to the surface and gives each speaker the feeling that his or her ideas are valued. It also encourages the speaker to add more and share other ideas, as you can see in the dialogues you've just read.

When you are listening actively, you can also communicate that listening through nods, monosyllables ("hmmm!"), and body language. Communication can easily be shut down by group members who use body language to pass judgment. Rolling your eyes, folding your arms, shaking your head, and turning away from the speaker are disapproving signs that we all know well.

Listening actively and nonjudgmentally may be especially difficult when you disagree with the speaker's ideas. However, you don't have to agree with the speaker; just make it clear that you have heard and understood what the speaker is saying. This is an important skill for teachers to use with their students, and these case discussions will give you opportunities to practice the technique. If you would like more information about the power of active listening, check the references at the end of the chapter.

Brainstorming

Many group-oriented systems give lip service to brainstorming, but few carry it out effectively. To get as many ideas into the discussion as possible, group members need to feel open about sharing. In true brainstorming, therefore, no ideas are evaluated until all the possible ideas are identified and put on the table. Once everyone has had a chance to contribute ideas and all attempts at new ideas are exhausted, *then* the evaluation process can begin with a healthy debate. Having to defend and explain your position is a powerful way to synthesize your own previous learning. Incorporating different perspectives can help us all see new ideas and issues that weren't at first apparent.

It may be helpful to come up with a system to make sure that everyone gets a chance to contribute to the discussion. One group member, on a rotating basis, might be designated to act as facilitator. The facilitator gently reminds group members to give everyone time to speak and encourages those students who haven't been heard from. A simple statement like "Let's hear what Deirdre thinks about this" can go a long way toward encouraging participation.

Settings for the Cases

These cases were written by students like you, as part of a seminar course taken during their final student teaching. The students represent the complete range of our teacher preparation programs: early childhood, elementary, middle school, and secondary education. The majority of the cases come from large, urban public schools, although some rural and suburban settings are also included. Student teaching lasted for 16 weeks. The first few weeks were mostly observational, with students helping informally. The student teachers gradually assumed more responsibility for planning and leading the class until they took over the class completely by the end of the semester.

Student teaching placements are arranged by a central office at our state college in conjunction with the central offices of school districts. The selection of the cooperating teacher is made by the building principal. There is too often a wide gap between college-defined good practices and student teachers' experiences in the schools. This tension is reflected in some of the cases. These students sometimes had to struggle with turning a less-than-ideal teaching placement into a positive experience when another placement was not available.

The students wrote their cases, shared them with other students in the class, and then edited them before handing them in. We think they are compelling stories of real classrooms and hope they inspire new ideas, stimulate cognitive conflict, and provide a deep sense of the complexity and excitement of teaching.

Sample Case Analysis

It may help to understand how case analysis works by looking at an example. As part of a curriculum course, we often use the case *Should We Celebrate Holidays?* The students all read the case before class, and the first thing we do is to just review what actually happened. We make a chart of all the people involved in the case and review the major events that lead up to the dilemma. It would look something like this:

People	Events
• Megan Loughlin—student teacher	• Megan assigns Halloween stories.
• Michael, Marissa, and one other student, none of whom celebrate Halloween	• Some students refuse to participate.
• Students at their lockers	• Megan gathers information on other religions/cultures.
	• Megan focuses on cultural study rather than traditional Halloween themes.
	• Students complain about not celebrating Halloween.

Next, we brainstorm what are the major issues that need to be considered in the case before we decide what the teacher should do. It is sometimes difficult to not jump right into solutions, but it's helpful to know what the issues are before being able to decide what to do. One way of getting all the students to participate is to start everyone off writing down on scrap paper as many issues as they can think of. When everyone has had enough time to write, we give each student a turn to read one item off his or her list. We post these on chart paper, going around the room again until all the ideas have been recorded. The list might look like this:

- Learning about other religions
- Can we teach religion in public school?
- Should kids feel left out?
- Parents' rights
- Cultural diversity
- Role of holidays in curriculum
- How to teach about other cultures
- Getting rid of all holiday celebrations
- Who decides what to celebrate?
- When parents and teachers disagree

Each one of these issues can be the basis for a lengthier discussion. Sometimes we work in small groups, with each group tackling one of these topics. Then each group spends a few minutes reporting back to the whole group. This point in the analysis is a good time to think about how theory and research inform our teaching. What readings have you done in your teacher preparation classes that are relevant here? What theorists shed light on these issues? For example, how would the more traditional psychological views of Erikson or Maslow apply here? How about postmodernist ideas? What other resources can you find that relate to multiculturalism?

The next step is to think of solutions. We have the students again work in small groups to come up with suggestions in two categories: short-term solutions (i.e., what should Megan do right now?) and long-term solutions (i.e., what should Megan do to prevent this, or to ensure a lasting solution?). Students will write their suggestions down and share them with the whole group when we reconvene.

When you come to this step during your own case analysis, we encourage you to think of similar experiences you may have had. Many of the issues in these cases are important ones for all age-groups. Imagine your own teaching situation and how this problem would affect you and the students you work with. You can also use the issues that are uncovered in these cases to write your own teaching case. This allows you to examine more closely a problem that is on your mind and, it is hoped, share it with your peers for feedback. Part III of this book gives suggestions for writing your own case.

To summarize, one problem-solving method involves the following steps:

1. Review the details of the case.
2. Identify the major issues in the case.
3. Identify theory, research, and other resources related to these issues.
4. Consider short-term and long-term solutions.
5. Relate the case to your own teaching.

Finally, we will remind you that teaching involves such complexity that no dilemma has only one right way to proceed or one solution. We hope that you will develop the ability to reflect on the many possible courses of action in your teaching and make thoughtful decisions.

For Further Reading

Derber, C. (1979). *The pursuit of attention: Power and individualism in everyday life.* New York: Oxford University Press.

This small book goes beyond most treatments of active listening by illustrating how gender, class, and other social divisions profoundly affect who gets heard and who does not. An awareness of how attention is distributed in society can help sharpen listening skills.

Faber, A., & Mazlish, E. (1995). *How to talk so kids can learn at home and in school.* New York: Rawson.

This very readable book, illustrated with cartoon vignettes, covers how to deal with students' feelings that interfere with learning, suggests skills to get kids to cooperate, discusses pitfalls of punishment, shows how teachers and students can solve problems together, demonstrates effective praise, suggests how to free a child who is locked into a role, and examines the parent-teacher relationship.

Gordon, T. (1974). *T.E.T.: Teacher effectiveness training.* New York: Wyden.

This classic volume has invaluable information on the teacher-learner relationship, how to avoid roadblocks to communication, guidelines and uses for active listening, how to handle students' problems, how to prevent problems, and resolving conflicts.

Rogers, K. R., & Farson, R. E. (1987). Active listening. In C. R. Christensen (Ed.), *Teaching and the case method* (pp. 166–174). Boston: Harvard Business School.

This essay defines active listening, shows how to listen actively, and suggests what to avoid.

Schön, D. (1987). *Educating the reflective practitioner.* San Francisco: Jossey-Bass.

This thorough volume promotes "reflection in action" as a way to improve professional development in education to meet the needs of the complex, unpredictable problems of actual teaching practice.

PART II
Cases from the Field

SECTION I

Challenges of Creating Classroom Communities

CASE 1

You're Not the Teacher!

Rosemary *Fontenot tries to get the children to see her as the "real teacher" while struggling to find a way to handle a difficult child. She wonders how effective she is at teaching kindergarten and what she should try next.*

"I don't have to listen to you! You're not the teacher!" screams Otis at me after I calmly let him know that I don't like to see him hitting the other children. He sneers at me and walks away. I look at the clock, and it's only 8:46 A.M. The students have been in the classroom a total of 60 seconds. It's going to be a long day.

After a day with Otis and his 24 classmates, I wonder how effective I am as a teacher. As I look around me, I realize that this kindergarten class is quite fortunate because the classroom is twice the size of any other room in the school. Most of the classes have up to 30 children with only one teacher.

The majority of students who attend Jacob Jones Elementary School are Latino, born of immigrant parents. The school offers many bilingual classes to help the students adjust. Many of the parents don't speak English; school correspondence is sent home in both English and Spanish. Sixteen of the 63 teachers teach their classes in Spanish. No one in the central office or in the nurse's office speaks Spanish, and neither the principal nor the vice-principal speaks the language. As of this year, there no longer exists a parent-teacher association.

The kindergarten children seem to know their routine: come in, hang up coats, and take seats. After attendance, lunch count, and homework collection, it's time to do the calendar. Most of the children raise their hands, saying, "I know! I know!" But Otis is usually turned in a different direction, and he's usually playing with something or bothering someone. If he does raise his hand, he just stares at me blankly when I call on him.

After the class returns from gym, music, or library, we usually learn a new letter. But when I pass out the books, Otis exclaims, "Oh, not books!" I have been in this classroom for seven weeks, and this is Otis's sixth month in kindergarten. When I first arrived, he did not know any letters. Then I helped him learn the letter *O*, as in his name, Otis. I was so excited; I felt so good about helping him. Since then he has learned another letter. I was sure that when he started feeling some success, there would be a difference in his behavior. I had hoped that maybe he would not be so mean and aggressive with me now that he was learning, but it hasn't happened. He continues to act out.

I have tried to keep Otis on task, but he is very defiant toward me. I've tried telling him how that makes me feel, and I've also asked the other children to explain to Otis how they feel when he misbehaves. Otis, however, will deny ever doing anything. I've tried praising him when he does something positive on his own or with some direction, and I've also tried to ignore the negative behavior and concentrate on the positive, but I still get, "You're not the teacher!" I don't know how to get him to see me as an authority figure and to develop respect for me.

Although I have full responsibility for the class now, I still feel like it is my cooperating teacher's class. I'm just not sure the children see me as a real teacher yet, especially Otis. For that matter, I'm not sure how much I see myself as a real teacher. Tomorrow is a new day, and I'd like to start out on a different foot. But what can I do to reach Otis?

Questions

1. How much of this student teacher's problem stems from the fact that the children do not see her as the real teacher? What are other possible reasons for Otis's behavior?
2. What are appropriate expectations for children's behavior in kindergarten? What child development theories would provide useful information for the teacher in helping Otis and the rest of this class?
3. What do you think about the strategies this student teacher has tried so far? What else would you do? Why?
4. What specific fundamentals of classroom management do you think are important to consider in this case before deciding what action to take?
5. What other information would you like to have about Otis before making a decision about what to do? How could you get that information?

CASE 2

My Creative Nightmare

Brianna is excited to try out a lesson that would foster creativity among her first-grade students while they are learning language skills. The lesson creates a great deal of noise and confusion that she didn't expect, and she is left without a backup plan.

I am assigned to a small suburban school with a mostly Caucasian, middle-class student population. My first week of school in September was exciting and fulfilling. I helped my cooperating teacher, Ms. Dalstrom, and the students when they needed an extra hand. I listened attentively while my cooperating teacher led lessons, and I observed her carefully. All the while I was thinking of all the creative, hands-on activities I had learned to do in my college classes. Most of the lessons I had observed so far were based on the many workbooks and textbooks that this first grade had to use.

I was thrilled when Ms. Dalstrom said, "Brianna, let's get you started right away. Why don't you prepare a language lesson for Monday?" I was glad it was Friday so that I would have the whole weekend to prepare. After hours of work, I was finally satisfied that I had ready an exciting, creative lesson.

Monday morning rolled around, and I began with a flannel board story of *Jack and the Bean Stalk*. My objective was to have the children listen to the story and retell it using pop-out puppets from their books to build language skills and an understanding of story structure. The flannel board story was great! The children were amused by my homemade characters, and they seemed to appreciate my knack for storytelling. After I read the story, I asked the class who could tell me what happened first, next, and last. The group was eager to answer, and they were on the money each time, so I knew that their comprehension was good.

Then came my wonderful creative activity. I had the children punch out the characters from the back of their workbooks. Then I assigned them to groups of four. Each person would have a chance to play each one of the four characters: Jack, the giant, Jack's mother, and the giant's wife. The children got into their groups, and the noise began to grow. I expected it to be a rather loud activity since all the children would be playacting, but I was unprepared for how loud it got. This was not a busy hum but a loud roar. I tried to circulate in and out of each group. The groups I listened to weren't retelling the story; they were making up their own stories. Some of the groups were arguing about what character each person was going to play. Some of the children refused to participate because they couldn't be Jack. No one wanted to be the giant.

The room continued to grow uncomfortably loud. As I was desperately trying to think about how I could get the children quieter and more engaged, my cooperating teacher whispered, "Brianna, do you have a backup plan for this lesson?" I hadn't thought of anything else for the children to do. In my mind, I had envisioned them intensely acting out the story for the whole time period.

Ms. Dalstrom suggested that the children could now begin to review the story sequence. I had no other plans myself, so I told the children, "Put your puppets away and go back to your seats now. Get out your workbooks and begin to color in what happened first in the story, next, and last." The children reluctantly put the puppets away and moved slowly back to their own desks.

I felt defeated. What happened to my activity? I put a lot of thought into it, but you couldn't tell from the results. The storytelling went well, but not my creative follow-up. What could I have done differently?

Questions

1. What do you know about classroom management that helps you to analyze the sources of Brianna's problem? How do routines, signals, the classroom environment, and communicating expected behavior relate to this case?
2. What short-term solution would you suggest when a lesson doesn't go as expected? How would you adapt Brianna's lesson? What long-term solutions do you think would help her students?
3. What are appropriate expectations for first graders' behavior? What do you know about their cognitive, social, emotional, and physical development that could help you plan creative lessons?
4. To what extent are worksheets and textbooks appropriate in first grade? How can you develop creative thinking when you are required to use such textbooks and worksheets?
5. Have you had times when your lessons did not go as planned? What did you do? What types of backup lessons are most useful? What have you learned from lessons that did not go as planned?

CASE 3

Attention, Please!

Miss Holmes tries a fun, interactive lesson with her first-grade class but can't seem to get the students' attention. She struggles to understand her classroom management choices and decide what will help her be more effective.

I was excited about student teaching in a first-grade class. However, given my prior experience, I was also a bit nervous about my classroom management skills. My previous fieldwork taught me that I needed to get more assertive with my students, but I did not want to resort to harsh methods that would instill fear in them.

Ms. Richards, my cooperating teacher, was supportive and gave me sufficient time to teach the class. The students had diverse abilities; therefore, during my lessons some of the students got the concept quickly, while others needed more time. What happened as a result was inevitable. The quick students became bored and restless, while others called on me for assistance.

To rectify this problem, I decided to incorporate a more fun and interactive way of learning. Since the class was learning about money, I created a classroom store with various objects for sale that were from the learning centers. Each student had money and took turns buying something. Once they did this, they took objects back to their seats. Surprisingly, this resulted in chaos and confusion and made me uncomfortable.

Once the students bought their objects, they began playing with them. I told them before the activity started that I would give them plenty of time to play with their objects, but that while the activity was going on I needed their attention and cooperation. This just did not compute with these 21 curious students. The students who had their items were distracted by them, while the others waited, none too patiently, for their turn. I realized that I needed to construct the activity in a better way. I wondered what I would do to get their attention.

I then remembered one of Ms. Richards's signals to get the students' attention. I said loudly and seriously, "One, two, and . . . three." Just as I realized that this was not going to work either, Christine, a clever six-year-old, said, "Miss Holmes, you used the wrong signal!"

I thought to myself, "I'm a failure! Why can't I get their attention?" I thought about ending the activity or taking the objects away from those children who were not listening. I did not know which would be the right response, so I continued even though I felt as if I had lost control. Afterward, Ms. Richards chided the students, "I was disappointed with how you all behaved during Miss Holmes's lesson. I expect you to listen and pay attention to her when she is working with you!" This only exacerbated my guilt because I knew that I, not the students, was the cause of the failed lesson.

I was overwhelmed with questions. "Was it the difference between Ms. Richards's and my style and demeanor? Did I need to get loud and tough as Ms. Richards had been with the students? What will I do the next time I teach?" The thought of facing them again terrified me. What would I do differently?

Questions

1. Based on your educational courses, identify some of the causes of Miss Holmes's difficulty with this lesson.
2. What characteristics of young children would you need to consider in redesigning this lesson?
3. To what extent do you think teachers need to be "loud and tough" to get the students' attention? What other options are there? What aspects of classroom management should be considered?
4. If you were a student in this class, what would you think about this lesson?
5. What role do the children's mixed abilities play in this case? What pedagogical decisions should be considered to meet the children's diverse needs?

CASE 4

I Tried to Be Their Friend

Miss Martin is in the second month of student teaching in second grade. She struggles with finding the right balance between being the children's friend and yelling at them so that she can gain control. How can she care about the students but not control them? How can she instill responsibility when they won't stop playing long enough to listen to her?

Well, it's the first of March, and I'm about two months into this student teaching situation. To say the very least, it has been interesting. Let's start at the most logical place—the beginning. I was placed, by request, in a school in a suburban area close to the shore, basically for transportation purposes. When I went to visit the school, I figured, "Wow! What a nice area! Nothing like the urban area where I carried out my observations." Of course, in that reaction was the assumption that the middle-class children here would probably be more easily managed than the urban students I had worked with during my junior field experience. In fact, I carried out the first three weeks of this student teaching internship thinking the same thing. Wake up, Miss Martin!

You see, I had wonderful lesson plans; even my cooperating teacher and supervisor loved them. I kept a notebook of all my plans and everything I'd like to show, tell, and do with the students. Yet I found out that the notebook doesn't mean a thing unless you have the children's attention, and that's what I didn't have and couldn't seem to get. I had been told in my teacher education classes that if the lessons were good, interesting, and solid, I would have the students' attention. I wish I could remember who said that to me. *They lied!* That might work later on in the semester, but it certainly wasn't going to work for me now.

I found I had all the usual problems that I understand student teachers encounter with their students: talking when the cooperating teacher walks out of the room, trying to get away with more when she's not there, and speaking differently to established teachers than to me. If I was going to get their respect, it was clear I had to earn it.

I started off with a big mistake. I tried to be their friend. I tried joining with them in all the jokes and laughter that cut into instruction time. When this didn't work, I overcompensated by yelling at them when I needed them to quiet down and get to work. I wasn't at all comfortable with this situation. I did not think it was like me to raise my voice at a child. I knew I needed to consider how they felt. I realized that if I were them, I'd hate me, I really would. In desperation, I turned to my education textbooks for advice.

This was a huge help to me, but a book can only guide you. It can't establish a personality for you or even manage your classroom for you. You have to do that yourself and as lovingly and effectively as possible. But I had so much trouble finding a middle ground: love them, guide them, talk to them, manage them, but don't control them.

I talked with my supervisor, an understanding, caring person who has a strong influence on me. She said, "Make the students responsible for the way that they behave. Tell them how you feel about what they are doing instead of dictating a punishment. Give them a choice about the outcome of their behavior." This was good advice, but easier said than done. Sometimes I can't even get their attention to explain how I feel or to ask them about outcomes!

My students have continued to cut up, especially when my cooperating teacher leaves the room. I have to admit that a couple of times the clowning around and refusal to get down to work has gotten so bad that I almost dropped out of teaching altogether. But I have also realized that in the few short weeks that I have been student teaching, these children have had such an impact on me that I can't give up. I won't. I want to teach.

I know that if this experience is to be successful, I have to use different techniques from those I've been using. The questions I have are, What will work in this class? How can I love these students but not control them? How can I really make them responsible or give them choices when they won't stop playing long enough to hear me?

Questions

1. Why do you think Miss Martin has difficulty getting the students' attention? What factors affect this problem? What advice would you offer Miss Martin?
2. Why do the children respond to a student teacher differently from the way they respond to the regular classroom teacher?
3. How do you feel about Miss Martin's assumption that suburban, middle-class children will not present the classroom management challenges of urban students?
4. Based on your classroom teaching experiences and your experiences as a student, what do you think about the balance between being a friend to the students and being the authority figure?
5. Have you gained new perspectives on what the concepts presented in your education courses now mean?

CASE 5

Class Out of Control

Ms. Leon experiences one of the worst days of her life when her cooperating teacher is absent: she cannot get control of the third-grade class and needs the assistance of the substitute teacher and the vice-principal. She wonders what she did wrong, what she could do differently next time, and whether she is cut out to be a teacher.

I was assigned to a large, urban grammar school for my student teaching. I was anxious to meet my cooperating teacher, Ms. Ahlberg, and the third–grade students. I couldn't wait to begin my student teaching. I felt that I was fully prepared to deal with any kind of situation, but unfortunately I was wrong.

Ms. Ahlberg was a teacher with 25 years of experience. I knew that I was going to be able to learn many things from her. I was thrilled to be introduced to the class on the first day as "Ms. Leon" as a classroom full of curious faces greeted me. In the first week, I was very impressed by the way Ms. Ahlberg conducted her lessons and by the way she handled the different classroom situations.

At the same time, there were often discipline problems. I felt that the way she arranged the classroom contributed to the problem as well as her very controlling attitude. Her classroom was not big enough for the 27 students. She divided it into two sections with two rows each.

During the second week of my student teaching, my cooperating teacher got sick. She called me early in the morning to let me know what she had planned for the day. The principal let me stay with the substitute teacher, Mr. Carson. I thought that this was a good opportunity to prove to myself that I was able to handle the classroom.

When the students walked into the classroom, everything seemed to be under control. Mr. Carson and I shared the responsibility of conducting the lessons. Mr. Carson gave them a long list of rules of behavior that they were supposed to follow. I thought that was fine for the primary grades. He seemed to be calm at all times with the students. Then he continued with the lesson, and I assisted him by working with the children that needed some help. My problems began when Billy refused to listen and do what the class was told. I spoke to him and explained that the teacher had given me the lesson plan that the students were supposed to follow, but he didn't understand.

When it was 10:00, I took the students to the bathroom. They started running, and I lost complete control of the class. I didn't know what to do or where to start to gain the control back. At that moment I truly believed that this was one of the worst days of my life. One of the teachers who saw what was happening assisted me by calling Mr. Carson. I continued leading the students downstairs, when they were screaming so loudly that one of the security guards came out and yelled at them. I felt very embarrassed. Finally, Mr. Carson came to help me lead the students back to the classroom. I felt some relief when he came to my rescue.

When we came back from the bathroom, Mr. Carson began conducting a lesson. Once again, Billy started acting out, distracting the classroom. I was getting frustrated by trying to control him. Finally, I gave him two choices: listen and follow directions, or go to the principal's office. He controlled himself for a few minutes, and then the bell rang for lunch.

When the class came back from lunch, all the children seemed hyperactive. I asked them to calm down and put their heads down. I turned off the lights for about three minutes. When I turned the lights on, Mr. Carson came back from lunch, and this time I started giving directions to continue the lesson. Everything seemed to be under control until Jorge and Danny started acting out. I couldn't take it anymore. I started yelling at them. I went over to their seats, but they were still not listening. When I turned around, Jorge got out of his seat and started running around the classroom kicking, punching, yelling, and cursing. This situation was out of control! One of the students told me that if I pressed the button on the wall, I would contact the office. Mr. Carson and I agreed to call the office and ask for help with the students who were disrupting the classroom.

After that incident, the vice-principal, Mr. Martinez, came to the classroom three more times to check if everything was under control. We also had the guidance counselor speak to the students who were misbehaving. Unfortunately, by now none of the students were interested in the lesson. Everything seemed to be upside down. What did I do wrong? Is this a signal that I should not be a teacher? What should I do next time?

Questions

1. What are some of the variables that could be causing the behavior problems in this case? What advice would you give Ms. Leon? What short-term solutions could she use to gain control? What long-term solutions?
2. Are there any hidden issues? Brainstorm as many as possible.
3. What aspects of classroom management that you have learned about are relevant to this case?
4. What do you think is Mr. Carson's view of the situation? Mr. Martinez's? Billy's? Jorge's? Pretend that you are one of the children in the class and give an account of what happened.
5. What do you think Ms. Leon sees as the teacher's role in the classroom? Do you agree? Explain.

CASE 6

A Special Bunch

Jill Harmon tries hard to establish a student-centered approach with plenty of opportunities for student interactions in her fifth-grade class. She struggles to deal with misbehaviors such as note passing during her lessons. She questions how she can be a supportive teacher and still correct misbehaviors.

On the first day of my student teaching in a small, intimate school of gifted children, I was informed by my cooperating teacher, Ms. Burch, that the students in this fifth-grade class were a special bunch. This became obvious to me during the early morning of the first class I taught. As I began my carefully prepared lesson, I watched five of the students continuously talk to one another across the room and pass notes discreetly. I definitely was faced with a problem that I didn't know how to handle. At first I said to the class, "I need to have everyone's attention on me during the lesson. When students are passing notes and talking, it is distracting for all of us." I thought that simply mentioning the situation to the entire class without making reference to any particular student might help. I added, "I just will not accept this type of behavior." I thought that by coming on strong without embarrassing individuals, I would gain the students' respect and attention, yet the talking and note passing still continued.

I thought back to my first week of observing this class. I had noticed then that my cooperating teacher did not make any reference to what was going on with those students who talked among themselves or passed notes. I am not sure if she simply was unaware of the situation, or if it just did not bother her. I know that she practices a student–centered classroom approach and allows the students to discuss their classwork freely with one another. But I also suspected that these students weren't talking about classwork as they whispered and wrote notes. So I was left in a cloud of confusion about how to deal with the situation while I was leading the class. After all, I, too, wanted a student-centered class in which the students would look toward their classmates for assistance. I felt this would enhance their learning and their socialization skills. On the other hand, I also wanted the class to know that I was really bothered by their actions.

As I continued to try to rectify the problem, I changed the seating arrangement. The next day, as I was going over the instructions for a science experiment, I noticed Sheila and Devon leaning over and whispering. I immediately stopped my presentation and said, "Sheila and Devon, you need to turn around in your seats and stop whispering while I am talking." Both girls rolled their eyes and slowly turned their bodies around in their seats. Neither of them made eye contact with me as I continued the lesson. Although the class was now quiet, I felt uncomfortable. As the students gathered the science materials they needed to carry out the experiment in their cooperative learning groups, I noticed that Theresa was passing a note to Sheila. Trying to hide my anger and frustration, I said, "Theresa, you need to get rid of that note now. You can come up and put it in the wastebasket. It is time to be working on science, not note passing." Although singling out the girls worked in the short term, to tell the truth I did not feel comfortable dealing with the situation as I did.

I didn't want to feel as if I was spending half the time handling misbehavior, but that's just what I was doing. I had learned in school to reach for student strengths, so I am trying to practice the strategy of giving the students a better attitude about themselves through praise. I explained to them that by correcting their behavior I was just trying to create a climate in which they could learn. I am trying to be a supportive teacher who still corrects misbehavior—always with the goal of redirecting students toward meaningful classroom work.

That same afternoon, I began to gather the students together for literature circles. I had four groups reading different novels. Today I was planning to have the students discuss their reactions to the first chapter and make predictions about the rest of the book. For the first five minutes or so, the groups were very productive, and I felt a surge of hope that all would go well. Just then, I noticed Devon lean back in her chair to pass a note to Theresa, who was in a different group. I wanted to shout across the room at them, but I kept my calm and tried to figure out what I should do now.

Questions

1. What do you think about the ways in which this student teacher tried to solve her problem? Would you have tried the same things? Why or why not?
2. Think back to your own experiences as a student and decide what might be the causes behind the student teacher's note-passing problem. What should this teacher do?
3. Do you think the cooperating teacher was simply ignoring the note-passing behavior, or was she unaware of it? Are there other explanations?
4. What theoretical assumptions about how children learn is this student teacher making?
5. In what ways are the age, developmental level, and gender of the students a factor in this case? What about the cognitive level of these gifted children?

CASE 7

Do Rules Work?

*__Carol__ Seaver, a student teacher in art, realizes that her junior high school stu-
dents are used to many different classroom management styles and tries to
develop her own techniques. She wonders why rules figure so prominently in
all the classrooms but seem so ineffective.*

I began my student teaching as an art specialist in a large, urban junior high school.
I am responsible for more than 1,200 students in a week. My cooperating teacher,
Ms. Merino, has been an art specialist for more than 25 years in this school system
and has given me a lot of insight into how art education has changed over the
years. She has been a great role model for me and agrees with my philosophy that
art should be interesting and fun for all students, integrated into all the subjects
that students study, and show students how art surrounds them in their everyday
life.

Our activities include multicultural non-Western art and interdisciplinary studies; we focus on multiple intelligences. For example, we play music and have the students visualize the various types of line that the piece represents, or we use visual aids
to help students with their projects. We also allow students to express their bodily-
kinesthetic intelligence by working in the manner that's most comfortable for them.

In this school, the art room has been taken over for use as a regular classroom,
and we travel from class to class teaching "art on a cart." Last spring I did a practicum
experience with this same teacher, and now I am back for a full semester beginning in
September. I was surprised to notice that the students act very differently in the
beginning of school than they did in the spring. The classes seemed much easier to
manage last spring than they do now! I have a better appreciation for how important
it is to establish classroom management during the first weeks of school.

There has been much confusion in the first few weeks, and Ms. Merino has
worked hard to define and teach the students the behavior she expects during art.
Most of the children (but not all) have a basic understanding of what is required to
create a productive, safe art class. After every lesson the two of us reflect on the lesson's
success and what needs to be altered to make it better. I have learned that a lesson may
be successful in one class and bomb in another. I think the success of a lesson can
also be determined by the class size and the classroom environment.

I know that cooperative learning groups are important for developing interper-
sonal skills, but they have been a problem because we don't have our own room.
Some teachers have the room set up so that the students are facing one another.
Others (we call these teachers spatially challenged) have cluttered, messy rooms that
can make the students or anyone coming into the room feel claustrophobic. As a

result, students talk constantly and ignore the instructions and the demonstrations. There are times when I can't get the students to cooperate and listen to instructions, so I move their desks into rows, the old-fashioned way.

After having read our college textbook on classroom management and considering my experiences at this school, I have come to a surprising realization about rules. I think they *promote* misbehavior. There is a prominent list of class rules in every classroom, but they don't seem to be at all effective. An example of this is one of the seventh-grade classes. All the rules are posted in the room as if they will be magically followed, but at 2:45 the same students are sitting in the gym for detention for talking too much, not doing their homework, and so on. Most of the students have been in detention since the first day of school and continue to have it every afternoon. It is obvious that the rules and this method of punishment are not working. I think the posted rules help set up negative expectations for students' behavior. It is almost as if they challenge the students to break the rules in a power struggle. Some teachers have the offending student write 100 or 200 times, "I will accept my responsibility." Writing something so many times does not solve the problem.

So as a specialist teacher, I have come up against two issues. My first question is, why do so many teachers post rules that don't work while ignoring the need to teach acceptable behaviors? My second question is probably one that all departmentalized teachers face: how do I deal with the diversity of classroom management styles that my students are used to while establishing my own techniques?

Questions

1. What do you think of Carol's assessment that rules promote misbehavior? What does she mean by that? Do you agree?
2. How do you think the physical environment of your classroom has affected r classroom management? What arrangement of desks or tables has worked r you? What has caused difficulty?
3. Do you think classroom management in a self-contained class is different f management in a departmentalized one? What techniques will help Carol establish her own style?
4. What effects of punishment have you seen in your own experience? Based on your understanding of motivation theories, decide what alternatives to punishment you could use.
5. How effective do you think "art on a cart" is? What types of art instruction do the students at your school get? How worthwhile is their art program? What evidence can you cite to convince others of the need for art instruction?

CASE **8**

I Want It Now!

Nancy *Shah is horrified when an angry seventh grader uses self-mutilation to get what he wants: to be able to go to the nurse's office for a medical form during class.*

As the fifth-period bell rang, I sat in the back of the classroom dreading the arrival of Ms. Nash's seventh-grade class, which I had just joined as a student teacher. Mind you, it wasn't that Ms. Nash's class was all that bad. In fact, most class members were quite the opposite, except for one student—Jimmy Blauser. Aside from being the class bully, Jimmy also seemed to be a pathological liar and manipulator. However, after witnessing what happened next in this class, I realized that Jimmy was taking his behavior to another terrifying level. It was time to acknowledge that Jimmy was a child in crisis and desperately in need of professional help.

Before fifth period, I sat in the teachers' lunchroom with my cooperating teacher, Ms. Nash, and Ms. Nevin, Jimmy's homeroom and third-period science teacher. Over lunch, Ms. Nevin warned us, "Jimmy might have a rather bad afternoon. You might want to be especially alert." Such discussions were quite frequent in the teachers' lunchroom. Ms. Nevin continued, "This morning during homeroom, Jimmy asked to go down to the nurse's office to get a form that needed to be filled out by his doctor in order for him to play basketball. He had already made the team but had to have a medical exam. Three other students had already asked to do the same thing prior to Jimmy's request, so I told them they couldn't go now but that I would find out about the form and either get them copies or tell them what to do about the form by the time they came back for third-period science. While this was fine by all the other students, Jimmy was furious. This is usually the case when he doesn't get what he wants immediately. Fortunately, the bell rang, and Jimmy had to leave for another class before he could blow up."

Ms. Nevin continued: "When Jimmy and his classmates returned for third-period science, I had the needed medical forms for them. When Jimmy did not come up to my desk to get one, I asked him why. He said he had changed his mind and that he was quitting the stupid team. I simply told him that it was certainly his right to do so. I was wondering if perhaps Jimmy, being so overweight, was worried that he would not pass the physical exam. Instead of running the risk of being ridiculed for not passing the physical, perhaps he took the easier way out."

Ms. Nevin continued her story: "Between the end of third period and the homeroom period before lunch, I ran into the principal and informed him that Jimmy had decided to quit the team. Given his numerous run-ins with Jimmy in the past, the principal was rather relieved to hear that he would not have to deal with conflicts between Jimmy and the other basketball players.

"When Jimmy arrived in homeroom, I told him that I had run into Mr. Paulsen and explained to him that Jimmy had decided to quit the team. Jimmy went ballistic. He shouted at me that I had no right to tell Mr. Paulsen. Jimmy then stormed over to his desk, threw his books on the floor, flopped down onto his chair, and stared at me with a look that could kill. After he had calmed down for a couple of minutes, he asked if he could have a medical form. I calmly said that I had already returned the leftover forms to the nurse. Jimmy demanded to go see the nurse. I said that it was time to leave for lunch and that I would try to catch the nurse during lunch and get him one. When the lunch bell rang, Jimmy bullied his way through his classmates and stood in line quietly fuming, glaring at me."

Having heard all this, I was not looking forward to the next class, which followed lunch. While my heart went out to Jimmy, who at the age of five lost his father in a terrible construction accident, I also couldn't stand the child when he went out of his way to take his bottled-up anger out on other students. I sat there hoping that Jimmy was over his anger as I watched Ms. Nash run through the math lesson. Not more than five minutes into the class, Jimmy suddenly stabbed himself in the hand with his pencil. Mute with disbelief, I started toward him. Jimmy jumped up, accused Kevin of stabbing him, and asked to go to the nurse. Ms. Nash immediately sent the bleeding Jimmy to the nurse while I calmed down the visibly upset Kevin. I then told Ms. Nash what I had seen. She asked me to take over the class while she went to speak to the nurse and the principal.

At the end of the day, Ms. Nash told me that Jimmy's hand would be all right and that Ms. Blauser had been called in to speak with the principal about Jimmy's behavior. Since Ms. Blauser had already defended her son's behavior many times in the past, often making what seemed like lame excuses for him or believing his lies despite eyewitness testimony to the contrary, Ms. Nash did not believe that she would be helpful.

"Were you able to find out why Jimmy stabbed himself?" I asked.

"I suspect he did it so that he could get to the nurse to ask for a medical form," she replied. "Evidently, after Jimmy had his hand looked at, he asked for the medical form. He even had a look of satisfaction on his face as she handed him the form." Ms. Nash added, "Jimmy obviously didn't want to take time away from his bullying at lunch in order to get the form from the nurse."

All night long I tossed and turned, thinking about Jimmy. Why would he mutilate himself to get what he wanted? Where was all his anger coming from? Couldn't his mother see that Jimmy needed help? Why was Ms. Nash acting so unfeeling about this incident? Why wasn't Jimmy getting professional help? What were we to do with Jimmy once he came back to class? Could he be a danger to other students?

Questions

1. If you were this teacher, what would you say to Jimmy's mother? What suggestions for professional help could you offer? What psychological services are available to the children in your school? Your community?

2. What classroom management techniques could you use to help Jimmy control his anger and behavior and not disrupt the rest of the class? How could the teacher's behavior affect Jimmy's behavior in a positive way?
3. What information do you want to know about Jimmy that you don't have in this case? What information would you ask his mother for? His pediatrician?
4. Retell this case from Jimmy's perspective. What do you think his view of the situation would be? How does thinking about his perspective help you meet his needs better?
5. What are some of the hidden issues in this case? Brainstorm as many possible sources of the problems as you can.

CASE 9

The Fight

Leslie *Jenkins begins her student teaching in an urban high school that has the reputation of being the toughest in the district. During her fifth week of teaching, her cooperating teacher steps out of the room. A few minutes later a fight erupts between two boys in her class.*

I walked Althea to the third floor of the large high school overlooking the harbor. The nervousness we both felt about meeting with the principal was beginning to wear off.

"Boy, that principal can really talk," said Althea as we made our way up the staircase, taking care to observe the school policy of keeping to the right.

"Yeah, I know what you mean. I guess he wanted to be sure that we know what to do in emergency situations."

"You're right. But I'll never remember all of the rules and procedures that he covered. I mean, who ever has time to think in emergencies? Confusing, really confusing."

We parted company. Althea went down the hall to teach a class on the Civil War. I walked in the opposite direction. As I walked through the dark and dreary halls, I thought about all of the warnings I had received from family and friends. I was told that this high school was the toughest in the district. Last year a student teacher was even assaulted by one of the students. I had also heard rumors that my college was considering canceling student teacher internships at the school. The high school had received bad press over the last few years and was supposedly dreaded by both teachers and students. But despite all the negativity that surrounded the school, I enjoyed my classes and my students. For the most part, my students were respectful and enjoyable. I thought that the school had a bad reputation that it couldn't shake.

I walked into my classroom. I was greeted by Ms. Green, my cooperating teacher, and we began talking about the unit that I was teaching. After Ms. Green offered her suggestions, she told me that she was going downstairs to the teachers' lounge to do some paperwork. For the past week, I had been left unsupervised in my classes, and, to tell you the truth, I actually preferred it this way.

The bell rang, and I began taking attendance. I was already in the fifth week of my student teaching and had built up an excellent rapport with my students. As I took roll, I noticed that Samuel was acting restless, twisting and squirming while looking at the clock behind him. I made a comment about his behavior as I continued to take the attendance. Samuel smiled nervously and seemed to relax somewhat.

I reviewed the work from the previous day. "Now if you'll remember, class, yesterday we reviewed the addition and subtraction of binomials. Today we'll learn multiplication and division of binomials. We're gonna have a lot of fun. I promise." The students laughed good-naturedly at my enthusiasm. I noticed that Samuel wasn't laughing but biting his fingernails and looking out into the hallway. When he became aware of my gaze, he shifted his eyes to his book.

I went on with the lesson. Then my words were interrupted by the noise of male voices talking loudly in the hallway. A crash vibrated through the classroom. It sounded like someone had slammed a locker door with great force.

I gritted my teeth and tried to proceed. All of a sudden I heard a deep voice yell, "There he is! There's the punk!"

A tall, muscular male looked into the classroom, noticed me, and shook his head to the others in the hall. He entered the class and moved quickly toward Samuel. The others followed him from the hallway. The first male violently pushed Samuel out of his chair and began hitting him.

I was in a panic. I knew that I couldn't leave to get help myself. I was unsure if I should try to separate the two boys or try to find the guard who was downstairs on patrol. The two classes next door to me were being covered by substitutes. I also wasn't sure if I would get my cooperating teacher in trouble by finding another teacher. I watched the two youths continue to hit each other. I realized that my own fists were clenched. I knew that I had to make a quick decision to prevent anyone from getting hurt.

Questions

1. How important is it for student teachers to know and follow school rules and procedures? Explain.
2. What is your district's policy about breaking up fights or other emergencies?
3. Should Ms. Green have left the classroom? What would you do if someone in authority expected you to violate school policy?
4. Explain Ms. Green's, the principal's, and Leslie's point of view. What can you learn by looking at each of their perspectives?
5. What should Leslie do in this situation? Was there anything she could have done to prevent this or to lessen the chance it will happen again? Have you observed fights or other forms of violence in school?

Case 10

On the Wrong Track?

Marcy Benjamin notices that Daniel, a bright student who acts out in class, may be bored. Because of his disruptive behavior and failure to do his work, the cooperating teacher wants to move him to the lowest track, something Marcy does not agree with. To complicate matters, the student teacher suspects that Daniel flirts with her.

I have been assigned to student teach in a wonderful 11th-grade English class. Thomas Paine High School is a large, somewhat traditional high school serving the small, rural surrounding towns in this county. Although I went to another high school, I live in this area and enjoy the fresh air and the closeness of the communities here. My cooperating teacher is Miss Parnell, and she has been so helpful to me. She lets me teach exactly how I want, and I feel as if I have been doing a great job helping my students become independent thinkers and workers and feel confident and secure about themselves.

I have one problem, though, as far as classroom management goes, and that is with Daniel. Daniel is an extremely intelligent boy. To me, he seems to be on a college level with his reading and writing. Although he never does his homework or seatwork and never studies, he somehow manages to get unbelievably high scores on all his tests. So far, Daniel may seem as if he belongs in the highest track here. Unfortunately, he is not. He is in the middle track. He is not in a class that is conducive to his exceptional mind because he has behavioral problems. He constantly yells out, distracts other students by making irrelevant comments, and even physically interferes with those around him as a last resort of getting the attention he is looking for.

I think that the reason for Daniel's behavior is obvious: he is bored and not challenged. Sometimes during a lesson, he pulls out a book from his desk and will block out everything else and start reading it to himself. I feel terrible that I have to tell Daniel to stop doing what he enjoys (especially when it's reading) and start paying attention to the lesson, which is obviously uninteresting to him because he already knows the answers.

I have noticed that sometimes when I talk about a poem or a story that interests Daniel, he will momentarily seem to be listening. On those days I feel so excited. I'll think that maybe I'm getting through to him after all, and isn't this what teaching is all about? Still, he continues to disrupt the class and doesn't really talk about the readings during our discussions. Even though Daniel does well on tests, my grade book is full of zeroes next to his name: for class participation, homework, and projects. I worry that he won't even pass this course.

Daniel manages to make very low grades in most of his other classes, too. I heard that he cuts his history class at least three times a week. Miss Parnell feels that Daniel is a hopeless case and has tried to get him moved to the lowest track because of his poor performance. She believes that he might be able to get the attention he needs there. I have heard that the teacher of that track, Mr. Cavaletti, is very good, but I can't imagine that Daniel will be getting the challenge that I think he needs. Recently, at open school night, Miss Parnell and I had a conference with Daniel's parents. They said that they wouldn't mind if he were moved out of the class. They said that the real problem with Daniel is that he is spoiled.

There's one more thing about Daniel that I don't understand, and I certainly do not know how to deal with. This concerns what I feel is his inappropriate behavior toward me. I think he may even be flirting with me. He makes remarks about the way I look, tries to catch my eye in class, and stands too close when I am talking to him. Daniel is a very large boy, taller than I am, and his actions make me uncomfortable. I don't really know if I'm imagining all this, and I don't want to hurt Daniel's feelings by demanding that he keep his distance. Maybe he just needs some positive attention and sees me as an ally. But I don't know what else to do. I care about his learning and would like to have something constructive to suggest about how to handle the situation, but I really don't have any answers.

Questions

1. Do you think students should be tracked in high school? Why or why not? How about in middle school or elementary school? Are the students you teach now ability grouped? What effect does that have on your teaching?
2. What do you know about the effect of tracking on students that can help you analyze this case? Do you think Daniel should be in a higher track? A lower track? A mixed-ability group? What are the advantages of mixed-ability groups for all levels?
3. If you were in Marcy's place, how would you grade Daniel? What is the policy in your school about grading? To what extent should grades be based on effort, achievement, or improvement?
4. If you were to have a conference with Daniel's parents, what would you tell them? How would you respond to their assertion that Daniel is just spoiled? What advice would you give his parents?
5. Is Daniel's behavior toward Marcy sexual harassment, flirting, or an innocent need for attention? What criteria would you use to decide? How do you think Marcy should handle her uncomfortable feelings about Daniel's behavior? How would your answer change if Daniel were 11 or 12 years old?

CASE 11

Profanity in the Classroom

Curtis *Parker, an African-American student teacher, wants to serve as a role model to his inner-city high school students but is frustrated by their use of profane language, which he believes will hold them back from future advancement.*

Today I strolled into Sojourner Truth High School with a bit of concern. I've been student teaching for the spring semester at the same high school I attended as a teenager and am really enjoying the experience, looking forward to it every day. Since February, I've been responsible for teaching five freshman world history classes to a group of inner-city students. The classes are made up of mostly African-Americans like myself as well as a small percentage of Caribbean, Hispanic, Asian, and Polish-American students. I care for these students and am committed to making a difference in their lives.

Ms. Callaway, my cooperating teacher, puts a lot of faith and trust in my approach to teaching. She told me that the students sorely need African-American males in positions of authority who can relate to their problems. She stressed that the students look up to me and enjoy my innovative lessons.

I know that I have in fact reached some of the students, and I am proud of my teaching successes. The students seem to be really learning by relating history to their everyday lives. I have spent many long hours trying to make history come alive for them. I want the students to see history as *theirs*, and I believe that I am meeting with much success, at least on the academic front.

But my zeal and eagerness are nevertheless starting to wear down. My growing lack of enthusiasm, I have realized, is due to the daily blatant disregard and disrespect that students have for themselves and others.

I find it difficult to teach a lesson without constantly reminding my class, "Watch your mouth!" "Take your hat off, please," and "Please be respectful of other folks' differences." All day long, in and out of class, I directly and indirectly hear conversations heavily laced with profanity, disrespect, and insults. I know that this kind of talk will not help my students advance themselves in the outside world. I know that for them to succeed, I need to help them gain self-esteem and to project a better image to others.

At first, I thought that maybe if I set a good example each and every day by using proper speech, not wearing my hat in the building, and respecting my peers and all the students, I could help. After all, I graduated from this same school and can serve as a role model of someone who has gone to college and gained a profession. But without fail, there was little improvement.

My failure to reach my students has caused me many sleepless nights. I worry that knowledge and love for history is not enough. So much is stacked against my students that they need every edge they can get. I remember Ms. Jefferson, a teacher at this very school, now retired, who inspired me to make profound changes in my own life. I want to do for my students what Ms. Jefferson did for me, but I feel that I am reaching a dead end.

One day, out of frustration, I simply asked the students, "Why do you think that it is *so* necessary to use profanity in the classroom?"

I listened to their answers: "It's a habit!" "It's the way I express myself!" "I can't help it!" "I don't know; it's the way I talk!"

So I went on to ask, "Why do guys wear hats in the building?" They pretty much all agreed that it was done "to be cool" and as a "habit."

"But how," I responded, "are you guys going to go to college if you are trying so hard to be cool all the time and can't control your mouths or your dress?"

They said they liked the way they talked and dressed and didn't need college.

Then I asked, "Well, why do you think that it's a must to insult or hurt someone's feelings?"

Everyone agreed that it was done because "it's fun."

"But what happens when someone's feelings are really hurt or the insults get out of hand?" I persisted.

"Well, I guess I got to kick his #>###**!" was the only response.

Deep down inside, I know there must be some hope for these kids, but I do not know where to begin or what else to do. I feel helpless.

Questions

1. Do you believe that it is a teacher's role to deal with issues such as profanity and dress? Why? Why not? What is your school or district policy on the use of profanity? What guidelines are there for students' dress, such as hats?
2. In what ways, if at all, would the situation have been different had Curtis been white or otherwise not understood the culture of his students?
3. Have role models inspired you in your educational past? If so, reflect on how they made a difference for you. How do you see yourself as a role model for your students?
4. How has the teacher's expectations affected this class, if at all? How much of a difference can Curtis's expectations for his students make? What else can he do to change his students' attitudes?
5. Should going to college be a goal for all students? Explain.

CASE 12

What Do You Do About Gangs?

Jason *believes he has seen signs that one of the students in his high school math class is a gang member. He is worried that he is stereotyping the students and also wonders what to do if it is true.*

I was scared to begin my student teaching in a high school on the East Side of this large, southwestern city where I've lived my entire life. I grew up in a mostly white middle-class neighborhood on the opposite side of town and hadn't really spent much time on the East Side, which is known for its gang problem. When I originally made my request for a placement to the director of internships at my college, I had specifically asked to student teach in my old neighborhood. But Ms. Kimball explained to me that she felt that I needed to have experience with diverse student populations, especially since most of the jobs for new teachers are on the East Side. So, once I learned what my placement was, I confessed to her that what scared me were the gangs. Instead of changing me, though, she cautioned me not to stereotype. She said teenagers were mostly the same everywhere and that if I wanted to teach high school, I'd better enter with an open mind to all students.

And actually, she was right. I was placed in a 12th-grade math class with Mr. Ward and found out right away that the students here at Cesar Chavez High School could be rowdy, but were basically good at heart. I knew at once that this was the profession for me. I felt at home here at Cesar Chavez and had a great rapport with the students. It may have been egotistical of me, but I enjoyed being liked.

Sometimes I thought Mr. Ward was a little too tough on the students, though. He was very demanding, sent students to the board to do their problems, and if anyone made a mistake he would stop the whole class and criticize them. At those times, I died a thousand deaths, because it was only a few years ago that I was in high school myself, and I knew it was important to keep your cool in front of your peers. Still, Mr. Ward always treated me in a professional manner, and I didn't have any reason to complain.

Sometimes the students told me things that they couldn't bring themselves to tell Mr. Ward. Jessica, for example, had awful monthly cramps and was out at least one or two days a month. You'd think Mr. Ward would have put two and two together, but he didn't. He'd just embarrass her when she came back to class and threaten her not to miss anymore. She came to me and told me about it, and even though I felt weird talking to Mr. Ward, I did. At first, he just scowled and said it was another excuse, but I did notice he stopped picking on Jessica.

My real problem, though, was Oscar. Oscar was just one of those guys that you had to love. He was so shy and gawky, but always tried to act tough. He wore the baggiest pants in the whole school, heavy chains, mirror sunglasses, and the same blue bandana every day. Usually guys like that scare me, but not Oscar, because it was so easy to see through him. Sometimes I'd look at his small, brown wrists poking out under the sleeves of his polo and just know that he never could hurt a flea.

The other guys in the class seemed to like Oscar, too. No one messed with him, not even the biggest bullies like Javier. In fact, students would whisper the answers anytime Oscar was put on the spot. And sometimes, when Mr. Ward wasn't looking, they'd catch one another's eyes, laugh, or pass each other M&M's. I saw a lot that was going on in that class that Mr. Ward just couldn't see. It's funny. The students did all kinds of things other than their schoolwork, and for me, it was plain as day. Mr. Ward, though, didn't notice.

One day while Mr. Ward was explaining an equation, I just happened to glance at Javier. I think it was because he was laughing a funny laugh. Anyway, I realized that he was looking in Oscar's direction, and I was curious as to what they thought was so funny. Oscar was bent over his desk, also laughing and looking Javier's way. Then I noticed it. Oscar had his hand under his desk. He was giving Javier a sign that I believed to be a gang sign. I was stunned. Oscar? Did this mean Oscar was in a gang?

It occurred to me right then and there that maybe Oscar and Javier were just kidding around and trying to act cool. Lots of kids did that. Maybe I was just stereotyping. I wondered, if the students involved had been white would I have had this same suspicion? In this school, we were supposed to report if we heard anything about gang activity, but I didn't know if this counted. I was a little afraid to bring this up to Oscar. If he were in a gang, he might retaliate in some way, though it's hard for me to picture it. And if he weren't, I would seem like a dork, not just to him, but to all his friends. Certainly I couldn't discuss the whole problem with Mr. Ward, because who knew what he would do? And I was afraid to even mention it to my student teaching supervisors for fear they'd think I was stereotyping. Still I didn't know what to do. What do you do about gangs?

Questions

1. Do you believe that this student teacher had a basis for bringing up the possibility that Oscar was in a gang to his cooperating teacher or student teacher supervisor?
2. What are some other options that the student teacher might pursue in handling this dilemma?
3. Do you think the student teacher would have had the same reaction if Oscar were white?

For Further Reading

Ball, S. J. (1990). *Foucalt in education: Disciplines and knowledge.* London: Rutledge

This book argues that schools, like prisons and asylums, are the sites of social control.

Developmental Studies Center. (1996). *Ways we want our class to be: Class meetings that build commitment to kindness and learning.* Oakland, CA: Author.

This practical book discusses why, when, and how to use class meetings to help K–6 students develop decision-making skills, create a comfortable atmosphere for learning, and build prosocial behaviors and attitudes.

Fennimore, B. (1995). *Student-centered classroom management.* Albany: Delmar.

This college-level text looks at classroom management in terms of the developmental needs of students and student empowerment. Strategies for management and perspectives on the lives of American children are included.

Foucalt, M. (1995). *Discipline and punish: The birth of the prison.* New York: Vintage.

Analyzes the prison system in France in the 1700s and sheds light on power relations in society and schools today.

Glasser, W. (1985). *Control theory.* New York: Harper & Row.
Glasser, W. (1986). *Control theory in the classroom.* New York: Harper & Row.

These two volumes discuss reforming classrooms and schools so that students have more interest, motivation, and control. The books provide a realistic view of how difficult teaching is and offer concrete ways (such as using learning teams) to help students gain control. See also *The Quality School* (Glasser, 1992) and *The Quality School Teacher* (Glasser, 1993).

Good, T., & Brophy, L. (1997). *Looking in classrooms* (7th ed.). New York: Longman.

This classic text provides tools for many aspects of effective teaching.

Kohn, A. (1996). *Beyond discipline: From compliance to community.* Alexandria, VA: Association for Supervision and Curriculum Development.

This book questions traditional classroom management, especially the notion that problems in the classroom are the fault of the students who don't do what they are told. The author presents a fundamentally different view: classroom communities instead of blind compliance. It's a book that will challenge most readers' assumptions about teaching.

Kohn, A. (1993). *Punished by rewards: The trouble with gold stars, incentive plans, A's, praise, and other bribes.* Boston: Houghton Mifflin.

A provocative challenge to traditional behavior management, this book presents research findings that show the harm inherent in many forms of rewards. It is a thorough volume that includes practical applications and suggestions for alternatives to rewards. Readers may feel threatened by Kohn's criticism but will be forced to rethink their assumptions about motivation.

SECTION 2

Challenges of Curriculum and Instruction

CASE 13

Creative Writing That Doesn't Conform

*   **Miss** Abbott's philosophy about how to teach writing differs from that of her sixth-grade cooperating teacher. This leads to conflicts during lessons and means that mixed messages are sent to the students.*

I was very enthusiastic about becoming a student teacher. I had worked at summer camps for the previous two summers and as a substitute teacher, so I was not worried about feeling uncomfortable around children. I was placed at a large suburban public school with grades ranging from kindergarten through sixth. My cooperating teacher, Ms. Gittinger, welcomed me with open arms. She had been teaching for more than 25 years and was loved by all of her colleagues and all of her students. She was a very patient and understanding teacher who hardly ever raised her voice. She tried to always encourage good behavior and positive attitudes and discouraged unacceptable behavior. However, I thought she was also a teacher who demanded control over the entire class and did not allow any room for the children to be creative or independent thinkers.

Almost immediately after beginning my student teaching, I observed that the physical environment of the classroom reflected Ms. Gittinger's intention to have total control. There were no learning centers in the classroom and only a small library table in the corner that the children were not allowed to use without specific permission from the teacher. Ms. Gittinger did not want the students to have to get out of their seats for any reason, so she arranged her class so that they never needed to. I did not agree with this method of management.

One of my first lessons was on creative writing. I was very excited about doing this lesson because I was an English major and I enjoyed creative writing. I felt that writing gave the children an opportunity to be part of their own learning experience. The children were asked to write a story about how things would be different if Dorothy returned to Oz for a second visit. They were given the freedom to decide where they wanted the story line to go and were encouraged to be as unique and creative as possible.

Although this freedom of choice was not something that the students were used to, their response to the lesson was amazing to me. I was impressed with the creative and imaginative stories that my class was coming up with. As the students were completing the first drafts of their stories, Ms. Gittinger and I walked around reading what the children had written so far.

I continued to encourage the students to be as creative with their stories as they could and told the children how well they were doing. After Ms. Gittinger had read a few of the children's papers, she told the class that they were being too silly. She basically wanted them all to write stories with a similar story line: Dorothy returns to Oz, revisits her friends, and that's all. In my opinion, this would make the stories boring. And to top it off, Ms. Gittinger was criticizing the same students' papers that I had just praised for their creative touch!

I stood by helplessly. Ms. Gittinger had given me control over the lesson, yet now I was not able to lead it in the manner that I felt was best. I was embarrassed because I was contradicted by Ms. Gittinger but also angry that I was interrupted in the middle of my lesson. I was confused about my own teaching methods and what to do next. I had been so sure that I was teaching the right way, but now I had doubts. Should I have continued the lesson in the mold of Ms. Gittinger even though I had a different philosophy? Should I have taught the lesson in my own way even though Ms. Gittinger did not support the students' creative efforts?

Questions

1. How important is it for students to have control in the classroom? What should they have control over? In what ways do you give control of the class to your students?
2. What is Ms. Gittinger's view of the situation? Retell this case from her perspective. What new information have you learned?
3. What are some things a student teacher can do when the cooperating teacher has a different philosophy? What are Miss Abbott's choices?
4. What can a teacher do when the principal or a parent has a different teaching philosophy? What possible courses of action can you come up with?
5. Have you doubted any of the teaching methods you have tried in your student teaching? Has your teaching philosophy changed or been strengthened in any way?

CASE **14**

A Dilemma Over Dittos

> **Dawn** *Myers, who is student teaching in fourth grade, is trying to work collaboratively with her cooperating teacher, who uses ditto packets as her primary teaching technique. Her college supervisor wants to see lessons with more active learning experiences, which Dawn agrees would be more effective. How can she meet the expectations of her cooperating teacher while trying to introduce different teaching methods?*

As I sat in my assigned fourth-grade classroom on the first day of my student teaching internship in a tightly knit working-class community, I enthusiastically observed how my cooperating teacher began the day. Nothing out of the ordinary, just the usual morning announcements, assignment of the monitor of the day, and finally the pledge to the flag. Next Ms. Davis, an experienced teacher with 15 years in the system, began a reading lesson. She introduced a story by first discussing the concept of synonyms and antonyms in the reading vocabulary. She then read off the reading vocabulary. These words were displayed to the class with a large magazine-type chart. At the end of the lesson, Ms. Davis asked the students to retrieve some ditto packets from a cubby. The class was to complete a worksheet on distinguishing synonyms and antonyms, which later was reviewed, corrected, and discussed. The students were also assigned a page from their readers on the use of synonyms and antonyms.

While observing this reading lesson, I felt it went smoothly in terms of classroom management, but I questioned its effectiveness. I noticed that students quietly complied with the teacher's instructions, but they did not seem enthusiastic, merely obedient. I wondered if this was Ms. Davis's usual teaching technique. I was soon to find out that my cooperating teacher's strategies did not change much from subject to subject.

For example, during one of her science lessons, she utilized a similar approach to teach the concepts involved in the body's functions. First, students read the section in their texts and were asked teacher-directed questions. Once the section was reviewed, she had the students again work on dittos independently for reinforcement and assessment. During our lunch break, I asked Ms. Davis about the lesson, "Can you tell me a bit about how you plan your lessons, and how you decide what to have the students do?"

Ms. Davis answered with confidence, "Well, reading the text passages is very important. They need to learn all the content in the textbook. The dittos reinforce what they have read and allow me to see where they are having trouble."

"Oh, I see," I mumbled, not sure what to say. This seemed so different from the teaching strategies I had learned in my college classes. But Ms. Davis was a teacher with lots of experience, and she was held in high regard in the school. Surely she knew what was best.

As I continued to observe Ms. Davis during the days before I assumed many teaching responsibilities myself, I realized that the students were very used to this pattern of lessons. At times she would have the students work on assignments cooperatively yet always on a worksheet. Ms. Davis mentioned one day, "These worksheets are so important in getting the children ready for the upcoming standardized tests. Since I have begun focusing so clearly on these ditto packets, my students have done extremely well on the tests."

I knew this was true because I had already heard it mentioned a few times that Ms. Davis's students had the top scores in the fourth grade last year. This began to worry me very much. I was certain that I would not become a "file cabinet teacher," just pulling out the worksheets each day, yet I knew that teacher accountability for standardized test scores is very important. I thought to myself, "What should I do about planning my own lessons for this class?"

When it came time for me to plan my first full lesson, Ms. Davis said, "Here is the teacher's guide and the dittos that I would usually use. Why don't you make it easy on yourself for your first lesson and just follow my lesson plan?" Because this was a math lesson, which is not my strongest subject, I said, "Sure, that would be a big help." Besides, I shared Ms. Davis's concern about the upcoming tests. What if student scores suddenly dropped because of my teaching? On the other hand, my supervisor, Dr. Clyde, was planning to come in today, and I strongly suspected she would be critical of a lesson that included worksheets. She had observed me in front of the class before, but this was the first time she would see a lesson that I had supposedly planned.

Because I was nervous and didn't want to offend Ms. Davis, I used her lesson as planned. I began the lesson with everyone at their desks, all eyes on me. I was so glad they were all paying attention. "Okay, everyone look at the board. Right here I have an example of an obtuse angle, and on the other side is an acute angle. Let me point out the differences." So far so good. I continued to explain the differences; and even when I mistakenly called an acute angle obtuse, Dr. Clyde merely smiled and nodded encouragingly from the back of the room as I corrected the error. But when I started distributing the dittos, I noticed her smile begin to fade, and she started writing on her evaluation sheet. I knew what she was writing only too well; I could have written it myself.

Afterward during our conference, Dr. Clyde shared what she had written in the space for recommendations: "I suggest devising 'active learning' exercises in which students explore mathematical concepts in pairs or in groups instead of relying on worksheets. I suspect these students are bored." I found myself mumbling again, "Oh, I understand what you mean." But by the time she left, I was confused and frustrated.

It's a week later now, and it is time for me to start taking over reading lessons, which Dr. Clyde will once again be observing. I'm not sure how I will develop my plans, but I don't want to just get rid of my cooperating teacher's dittos. I think it might even be best to continue with her lessons since the children are accustomed to them. At the same time, I want to respect my supervisor and try to teach the way I was taught by my college professors. This is a dilemma I'm sure I wouldn't have to face in my own classroom, but for now it feels like I must make a tough choice.

For my first reading lesson to plan on my own, I have been assigned poetry. The teacher's edition has many creative writing ideas, some of which I would enjoy using but which probably won't help the class on the upcoming tests. I still feel compelled to follow Ms. Davis's ditto format, even if I wouldn't choose to do this in my own classroom. After all, it is her classroom, the children are used to her, and I want her to approve of how I'm teaching. It's already close to midnight, and I haven't made a decision yet. I'm tired and confused, and I wish someone would just tell me what to do tomorrow!

Questions

1. How do you feel about the demands to please both your cooperating teacher and your supervisor from your college or university? Why are there sometimes conflicting expectations?
2. In what ways have you been able to successfully develop your own teaching style and philosophy in the face of differing viewpoints?
3. What role has standardized testing played in the curriculum choices made in the classroom in which you are working? How do you feel about the notion that tests drive the curriculum? What role has assessing students played in your student teaching experience?
4. What role, if any, do you believe that the socioeconomic class backgrounds or culture of the children at this school played in the kind of education they received? Was your own education similar or different?
5. What role should textbooks and worksheets play in curriculum planning? How can they be used most effectively?

CASE 15

Low Expectations

***Alicia** Cuervas questions her school's policy of ability grouping fourth graders. She sees big differences in the expectations for each group and wonders how she can challenge the lower ability group in her position as student teacher.*

I am doing my student teaching in a fourth-grade class in a large urban setting that draws together children from different backgrounds. Overall, the experience has been great. I bonded with the students right away. I was amazed that they so readily accepted me as their teacher and seemed to respond to my positive remarks about their work.

My cooperating teacher is Ms. Watkins, who is known throughout the district as a strong teacher. Many of the more affluent parents, in fact, tried hard to get their children into Ms. Watkins's classes. They were in agreement that their children consistently fared better in the fifth grade if they got her for a teacher. She was known as tough but compassionate.

In general, I consider myself lucky to have the placement I do. The school has a good reputation, and I know that a recommendation from here wouldn't hurt me at all. Besides, I had a lot to learn from Ms. Watkins's teaching style.

However, there are a few problems. One problem I have involves ability grouping. For most of the day, I teach Group 1, half of the class, while the other half, Group 2, joins with half of the other fourth grade. The only times I have the whole class are for homeroom, language, specials, and lunch. My problem arose one day when Group 2 entered the room and saw what Group 1 had been doing. One child questioned me, "Why can't we do that?" which seemed to reflect how all the children felt about being in Group 2.

I was especially interested in one student, Janine, who seemed to me to be very bright but to have difficulty staying in her seat and waiting her turn to talk. I guess you would say she had a behavior problem, but I really didn't think Janine should have been in the lower grouping. And besides, I didn't think that grouping on this basis was really helpful for anyone.

Not surprisingly, it was Janine who led the way in asking why Group 2 was so far behind. "Group 1 gets to use the computer when they finish their work, but we have to sit quietly," she would complain loudly, and her group mates would nod or speak out in agreement. "Why does Group 1 get to choose whatever books they want for their book reports, and we can't?" "Why are they working on long division?" "Why can't *we* go on the field trip?" Nothing seemed to escape Janine's notice. The questions went on and on, and, to tell you the truth, I was at a loss for answers.

I decided to raise this issue with Ms. Watkins. I asked her why there was such a division in the fourth-grade classes. "Wouldn't a mixed-ability group help everyone?"

Basically, Ms. Watkins told me that Group 2 could not do the same level of work as Group 1. "They just can't handle it," is how she put it. "You know, they don't have the background. You have to go much slower with them."

I did not argue with my cooperating teacher. I knew that she was under pressure from the principal and the parents and that she had experience that I did not have. Still, I worried. Group 2 members, I realized, knew they were at the bottom, and Group 1 members knew they were the "smart ones." Even though Ms. Watkins seemed to think that Group 2 members did not really know they were in groups according to their ability level, I noticed that when students asked, "Why can't we do what Group 1 just did?" another group member would quickly say, "Because they're smarter." Or when they would ask, "How come Group 1 is ahead of us in the story?" they would answer their own question: "Group 1 can move faster because they're smarter." I thought to myself that Group 2 members certainly knew the difference between the groups and wondered why my cooperating teacher treated them like they didn't have a clue.

Group 1 members knew there was a difference, too. The subject usually came up when they received work that I guess they found to be too easy. They would say, "Why do we have to do this? Isn't this for Group 2?" Then they might look at one another and laugh. At other times, Group 1 members would look at the homework board and know they were ahead and why.

This situation really bothers me. If my cooperating teacher expects me to do specific things with each group in a certain way, how can I go against that in her room? I want the children in Group 2 to know that I have high expectations for them and believe they can achieve as much as the Group 1 members, but every time I suggest something challenging, Ms. Watkins says they can't do it. How can I help these children feel equal when the school management calls for this kind of grouping?

Questions

1. What role do you think teacher expectations play in learning? Explain in detail, drawing upon your own educational autobiography. What have you learned in your education courses that could help you answer?
2. Do you believe that faster students are hurt by mixed-ability classes? Why? Why not?
3. What do you think should be the stance of student teachers toward institutional constraints that conflict with their teaching philosophies? Is it any different, in your opinion, for experienced teachers? Explain your answer.
4. What options does Alicia have? What would you do in her place?
5. In what other ways can a teacher tailor instruction to a variety of ability levels besides ability grouping?

CASE 16

Rush, Rush, Rush: How Can I Find the Time?

Darleen Jackson wants to be creative in designing lessons for her eighth-grade class but finds that there is not enough time to carry out her ideas. There is too much to be covered in the set curriculum at her school. How can she find the time to be creative and still cover this curriculum?

Textbook, workbook, textbook, workbook—I want to break the boring cycle! But how? There's not enough time to break away. How can we make time when we have to follow a set curriculum? We must cover a set number of subjects in a specific time frame. This is my problem.

Well, let me take you back to the beginning: college. I learned in my college classes about cooperative learning and being creative in the classroom setting. That sounded great to me. I was ready for my student teaching and nearly bursting with all my creative ideas! But I found that teaching was a whole other ballgame once I got into the classroom.

I was assigned to P.S. 3, a K–8 school near my college. I had asked to be placed in this school because I had heard wonderful things about it. Students' test scores are some of the highest in both the district and the state. I really didn't expect to get into P.S. 3 because the competition to student teach here is so stiff. Yet here I am.

My cooperating teacher, Ms. Jacobson, is great. She's open to all of these new, creative ideas I'm bringing from college, but she insists that we do not have time to linger. Every time I think of something fun to do, she compliments me but points out that we need to move on. This was something I didn't expect; the pace here reminds me of New York City. Rush, rush, rush!

I am definitely not a person who thrives on a hectic pace. I believe that it takes time to truly learn. In all of my college classes, I spent outside-of-class time reviewing what we'd been over for the day. I've always enjoyed sitting back and just thinking. At this school, though, you can't stop and think. It's just too busy. I think the time constraints do not let the children explore and learn at their own speed. Learning is actually fun, if only we let it be.

What really bothers me is that very few of the exercises in the texts are fun or encourage the children to think for themselves. I keep wondering why we can't forget the text sometimes and make up our own lessons for a change. That might motivate the students to get interested.

I think the real problem here is that we have a curriculum to follow. We plan for the curriculum, not for the learners. So where does this curriculum come from? Who puts it together? Well, in my district, Ms. Jacobson was assigned to join with another teacher and write the curriculum for this grade, aligning it with our state core curriculum standards. The two teachers admit that they did not have experience in writing curricula. They basically copied from the teachers' manuals of the textbooks.

But I wonder if it's any different anywhere else. Ms. Jacobson told me that the reason coverage is so important is that the students have to perform really well on their tests or else she'll get into trouble with the parents and the principal. As it is, she has an excellent reputation, and the scores are high.

One thing's for sure, Ms. Jacobson has had many years of experience in teaching, and I have none. I wonder if she had all of these great plans when she started out and then had to give up her ideals once she was faced with the demands of the test. She may be right that I tend to lag and answer every single question before going on. Maybe taking time to ensure that students are really learning does mean that they'll miss out on a lot of material in the long run.

I know these tests are given throughout the state, so I guess I'm not alone in having to cope with a set curriculum that is geared toward the tests. But I can't help thinking that while it may help some students be able to come up with the information for these tests, they aren't really learning much in depth. They end up bored, and so am I.

So all this leads me to ponder how important this curriculum really is. Do I continue to follow such a curriculum, or can I change my classroom? Must I follow the textbook-workbook cycle? If I teach the way I want to, how can I explain to Ms. Jacobson, the principal, and the parents that I didn't have enough time to finish what was supposed to be covered? How can I find time in the classroom to be creative and cover all that is in the curriculum?

Questions

1. Think back to your educational past. What do you remember learning? What were the kinds of curricular experiences that most clearly led to meaningful learning for you? What are their implications for your own teaching?
2. Explain the student teacher's dilemma from Ms. Jacobson's point of view. From the principal's point of view. From that of the parents. What have you learned from looking at these different perspectives?
3. What do you think about curriculum standards set by the government, district, and school? How can you teach for understanding rather than simply covering material while still meeting curricular standards?
4. What experiences have you had in pacing your lessons or your coverage of curriculum topics? Do you feel you have enough time?
5. What other solutions can you think of to have more time in the classroom, besides covering less in the curriculum?

CASE 17

Teaching or Test Preparation?

Melanie *Brooks is struggling with the contrast between the exciting, creative teaching methods taught in her college courses and the skill-and-drill curriculum used in her urban seventh-grade class to prepare the students for upcoming state standardized tests.*

I have been doing my junior practicum, which is my first extended teaching experience, one full day per week in a seventh-grade class in an urban middle school for the past two months. To my dismay it has filled me with doubt and confusion about the realistic world of urban teaching. There is a sharp contrast between the exciting, creative teaching methods we discuss and learn about in our college classes and the actual curriculum required and the textbook-driven lessons that are prevalent in the classes at this school.

The classroom I am assigned to is a reading and writing class, in which, as the teacher informed me, more than half of the students are reading and writing below grade level. Due to their history of poor performance on standardized tests, they will be taking the Early Warning Test (EWT, a state-mandated assessment usually given in eighth grade) in seventh grade and again in eighth grade to identify areas of weakness they need to work on for the High School Proficiency Test (HSPT). To my disappointment, their daily reading and writing lessons focus on EWT booklet activities and worksheets that reinforce the skills that will be tested. There are no creative writing assignments, no interesting topics discussed while reading an exciting story, and none of the cooperative learning activities I so frequently discuss in college workshops.

After two or three weeks, I began to wonder if I was just unlucky and was placed in a classroom with a teacher who lacked passion and creativity. After the third week, I asked my mentor teacher if it would be OK to observe other seventh-grade classrooms to get a feel for how other subjects are taught at the school. I was disappointed once again. Science and social studies were taught by the same teacher, who merely had the children read from their textbooks and answer questions from the end of the chapter. I did, however, see a slight improvement in the math teacher for part of the class. She had the students working on problems and analyzing solutions as a group. The other half of the class consisted of reinforcement activities worked on independently from the textbook.

The following week I once again reported to my assigned classroom and had a discussion with my mentor teacher regarding her lesson plans. She had attended a reading and writing workshop the previous week and explained to me how the instructors told the teachers the importance of making lessons interesting and relevant to the students' interests—for example, allowing the students to bring in magazines, books, or articles that they find interesting and create a writing lesson based on that. She told me that those ideas sounded "all well and dandy" but that, realistically speaking, if she were to use ideas like that in her classroom, her students would never cover all the curriculum standards required by the state, which in turn would affect their EWT scores. That statement left me wondering if all of the interesting and exciting methods of teaching I'm learning in my education courses are only used in model schools with ideal students. What happens to active learning experiences that require time for experimentation and investigation in a school where covering all of the curriculum requirements and improving scores on standardized testing is the most important aspect of the administrators', teachers', and students' future?

Questions

1. How important are standardized tests in the school in which you are teaching or observing? Do you think you are spending an appropriate amount of time, if any, in test preparation? What do the teachers at your school think and say about preparing their students for such tests?
2. If you were teaching in this school, how would you balance the need to have students perform well on standardized tests and the need to make the curriculum creative and exciting? Is it possible to engage your students in active learning that also enables them to get high scores on standardized tests?
3. Do you think standardized tests are important? How would your answer change based on the grade level of the students? What are the pros and cons of standardized testing? What would schools be like if there were no standardized tests?
4. To what extent have your classroom experiences reflected the philosophy and teaching methods espoused in your college or university classes? Why do you think there is sometimes a discrepancy?
5. What are viable alternatives to standardized testing? What types of alternative assessment have you used or observed? What are the pros and cons to alternative assessments?

CASE **18**

What Can I Do About James?

Melinda *Mora wants to make the most of her student teaching assignment in a seventh-grade classroom but believes that one student who is new to the district, James, is making it difficult for her to develop her skills as a teacher. While her cooperating teacher agrees that James needs to be evaluated, Melinda still must cope with his disruptive activities until the best placement for him can be determined.*

In my middle-school class of 25 seventh graders, there is a tall youth with an extended forehead, eyes that roll occasionally, scrapes on his cheeks, and quick and clumsy movements. James is part of a diverse urban school setting of Hispanic, Asian, African-American, and Caucasian students. He lives in a single-parent household where his mother abuses both alcohol and drugs. This is his first year at our school. He has already been to five different schools, and my cooperating teacher, Ms. Schumann, said that she really didn't get much information about him from his previous school.

James has difficulty responding positively to me as a student teacher as well as to the other students in the class. He is inattentive when we are reading and cannot respond to comprehension questions. When I ask a question, he will yell out to me, "Miss Mora! Miss Mora!" But he never has the answer. James often is moved to a desk at the back of the room as a result of his disruptive actions. He refuses to sit up straight in the chair and enjoys tapping his feet and loudly repeating certain words that I have said. He makes noises with his pen on the desk without respecting my need for him to calm down and be attentive. James often goes up to the front of the room to sharpen his pencil, wandering around the classroom while a lesson is being taught and making loud sounds while Ms. Schumann is talking. He uses his hands and legs in many negative ways, putting his feet up on the desk in front of him, pushing and tripping other students, and grabbing their clothing.

"Aren't these the behaviors of a young child?" I ask myself as well as Ms. Schumann.

"Yes, they really seem to be," she answers. "We have already sent home a note asking for his mother's permission to have him evaluated by the child study team, but we haven't heard from her. I hope she gives her permission soon."

James responds to the other students in a variety of attention-getting ways. One day during lunch period, I saw him aggressively grabbing Malcolm, another student in his class, to get his potato chips. Later I saw James talking and laughing with the same boy. After lunch, when James was supposed to be doing seatwork with the rest of the class, he tried to stick Malcolm with the point of his pencil. When I quickly intervened to remove the pencil, he angrily grabbed my wrist.

James's actions are often distracting to the class as a whole, especially when he refuses to participate in an activity and wanders around the classroom. The other students often say, "What is James doing?" or "Look at him." James does not speak in sentences or clear phrases and has a limited vocabulary. His speech is slurred, and each of his spoken words carries both a high and a low pitch. He often loudly calls out, "Look" or "Come here," requiring me to walk to his seat to discover the problem. "Could James be deaf and be able to read lips at times?" is a recurrent question that runs through my mind.

One day during a free period, I watched James looking through a comic book. He exclaimed, "Look, Miss Mora," and I stood beside him to see that he was pointing to a two-syllable word as if he didn't know it. I suddenly realized that he might not be able to read. "How did he get this far?" I wondered. I have noticed, though, that there are some simple words that he is comprehending.

One morning, in particular, stood out for me. The students were working on an activity at their desks. Prior to the activity, I demonstrated some of the concepts on the board. At that time all of the students showed their understanding except for James. I tried to get him involved but to no avail. He continued to wander around the classroom and went to the bathroom twice. I also found it hard to keep the attention of a few other students who watched James curiously. When I began to pass out sheets for the activity, James went to his desk. I thought, "Maybe now he will focus his attention and begin learning."

After writing his name on the sheet, he loudly called out, "Come here, Miss Mora." I quickly went to his desk, thinking that he might be interested and ready to complete the task. I explained what he needed to do and helped him with the first example. As I left his desk, I began to walk around the room, assisting other students in need. But James continued to call out, "Come here." At one point I realized that I must have gone to his desk about five times, each time finding myself directly showing him how to do the activity but not able to explain the task so he could possibly proceed independently.

When the period was over, I checked the completed activity sheets of each student. Of course, one student's paper remained undone: James's. When I looked at him, I saw that he was starting to shred the activity sheet into small pieces that were floating to the floor. Could he be angry because I could not constantly be at his side? I grabbed what was left of his activity sheet and asked him to finish it at home. At this moment, I found myself wondering what I could have done to help James complete that task or get the skills he needs to be even minimally successful. I am still quite uncertain about how to meet his needs as he remains a part of the classroom.

Now I realize that James really cannot process information about lesson content or guidelines of the classroom. To me it seems like Ms. Schumann tries to ignore James and consequently his needs. I believe that there is more we can do to help him until the school's child study team begins to assist. I guess because this is finally my chance to make a difference in students' lives, I don't want to believe I can't help. I feel that my philosophy that each student is unique and capable of growth should be expressed in my student teaching as well as in my future classroom. Most important, I know that my experiences and interactions with each student (including James) as a student teacher help shape my role as a caring teacher. Meanwhile, I have a whole class that's waiting for me. What can I do about James?

Questions

1. What are the referral procedures for students being considered for the special education program? What are the requirements? If you were to have a conference with James's mother, what would you say? How would you ask her to give permission for James to be tested? Do you think parents should have the right to refuse having their child evaluated or classified?

2. How do you think James could have gotten to seventh grade while still having such difficulty in reading? What factors have contributed to this problem? Do you think he should have been retained in earlier grades? What do you know from your coursework about the effects of retention?

3. What advice would you give Melinda Mora about helping James? Have you had students in your class that are functioning below grade level? Students that have been retained one or more years? How do you handle this? In what ways can you individualize instruction?

4. In what ways, if any, do classroom management and curriculum contribute to James's difficulties? What do you know about classroom management that would help you meet his needs while still maintaining an effective learning environment?

5. Would your suggestions for this case be different if the students were younger? What do you know about the development of adolescents that would give you insight into this case?

CASE **19**

Cooperative Learning: Trials and Tribulations

> **John** *Williams, a student teacher in a large, urban high school, tries to imple-ment a cooperative learning lesson that had been a big success in his college methods course. As he drowns in a sea of students' questions and hesita-tions, his confidence begins to crack.*

I was excited! I couldn't wait until my third-period class. I had spent the entire week-end devising a lesson that would really enable the students to interact with one another. I glanced up at the clock in the teachers' room of the large, urban high school that is my student teaching placement. I had another 15 minutes. I gathered my notes and materials. I was confident that this was going to be an excellent and enjoyable lesson for the students as well as for myself.

For the past two days, I had racked my brain to come up with a way of teaching my science class about some of the various forms of natural power that exist. Finally, I was satisfied with a lesson using cooperative learning that I had learned in one of my methods classes at college. Although my students, a diverse group of inner-city teenagers, weren't accustomed to cooperative instruction, I was positive that interac-tion was vital in the urban classroom.

While I had learned many of the technical aspects of instruction from my coop-erating teacher, Ms. Lam, I found that her teaching mostly consisted of lectures and worksheets. Although Ms. Lam had an excellent relationship with her students, I believed that the class needed more peer interaction. My education courses at college emphasized the benefits of cooperative learning, so when the time came for me to implement my own lessons, I was looking forward to trying it.

I decided that my lesson would consist of an activity known as expert grouping. For this activity, students are assigned to specialty groups to discuss what they have learned about a topic covered in class, which, in this case, would be natural power supplies. I separated my class into solar, wind, and hydro groups. After these groups met, students would return to a home group in which they would each report what had been discussed in their specialty groups.

I was very confident about this activity. I had done this kind of lesson as a final project in one of my college teaching classes, using fellow student teachers, and it was a complete success. So, much like I did in college, I began the activity on Friday to get the groups prepared for the work they would be doing the next week. On Monday, I wrote the names of all the students on the board. I gave the class instruc-tions, asked for questions, and immediately let students begin working. Before the class was five minutes into the lesson, however, several students raised their hands.

"Mr. Williams, someone from our group is absent. What do we do?"

"Mr. Williams, Charlie says he's not going to take notes."

"Mr. Williams, how are we going to get graded?"

"I don't understand why we have to do this. Ms. Lam doesn't make us do this kind of stuff."

"Mr. Williams, Simone wasn't here on Friday. She don't know what we did."

"Neither does Sandy."

"Neither does Kalil."

I tried to help each group individually but felt like I was drowning in a sea of questions. I didn't realize that a third of this class had been absent on Friday. I quickly grew very nervous. My confidence was cracking, and I desperately wanted the bell to ring so that my class would be dismissed. What should I do now?

Questions

1. What are some of the possible sources of John's problem with cooperative learning? Have you used cooperative learning techniques in your own teaching? What have the results been?
2. What could John have done to prevent some of the sources of this problem? What action should he take now?
3. Do you think cooperative learning is worth the time and effort? Why? Why not? Read some outside sources on cooperative learning, and see how the information could help John (or anyone in this position).
4. What role does the developmental level of the students play in this problem? Would you expect teenagers to behave differently from elementary students in cooperative learning activities? In what ways?
5. Do you think John would have experienced this problem in his own classroom, or was it a function of his being a student teacher? Defend your answer.

CASE **20**

To Lecture or Not to Lecture

Ralph *Spitler is discouraged by his cooperating teacher from using group activities or assigning homework in his high school history class because the students are low achievers.*

After all the preparation from college classes, I thought I was absolutely ready for student teaching. I believe I have an easygoing attitude, and I never anticipated having a problem during my student teaching assignment. I especially did not expect to disagree with my cooperating teacher.

I am student teaching in an American history class in a suburban high school that draws together diverse students from both affluent and poor families. The high school employs a strict system of tracking in all academic courses.

For two weeks, I observed my cooperating teacher. I watched Mr. Gant closely and made notes on how he conducted his class. Mr. Gant's style was much different from the way I had learned to facilitate a class. The students in Mr. Gant's class sat in rows and listened to the teacher lecture for the whole period. When the bell rang, they got up from their seats and left the room without any closure or homework assignment.

When it was finally time to take over the class, I naturally had butterflies but was eager to start teaching. I started my lesson with a brief introduction on the causes of the Civil War, then broke the students into small groups for an in-class assignment. The students were a little difficult to manage, but the class did not get out of control. Some students actually appeared to be enjoying themselves. I finished the class by touching on the key points of the lesson and giving a reading assignment for homework.

After the class, Mr. Gant and I discussed the conduct of the class. Mr. Gant told me that these students were low achievers and that group work was not really suitable for them. He also told me not to assign homework because the kids would not do the work. This advice was somewhat disturbing because what Mr. Gant told me went against what I had learned in college. I did not let this discussion discourage me. I decided to continue conducting my classes the way I felt was best.

The next day, I planned a hands-on collaborative project, a construction of a timeline based on the assigned reading from the night before. As Mr. Gant predicted, the students had not done the reading. I went ahead with the project and explained what to do as they went along. Again, the students were excited, rowdy, and difficult to manage, but their behavior was nothing that I couldn't handle. The project went slowly and took up the entire class time. The remaining work not covered in class I assigned as homework.

After class, Mr. Gant had another discussion with me. He told me that these students would never behave in groups. He suggested I go back to "good old basic" teaching because I could cover more information that way. Mr. Gant said that he knew the students would not do the homework. He implied that I should forget what

I had learned in school; this was the real world, and besides, this class was made up of slow learners.

That night at home, I reflected on student teaching so far. It was true that the students had been quiet and polite for Mr. Gant and that all of the material had been covered. Mr. Gant had many years of experience as a teacher, and after all this was the real world of teaching. But should I so drastically change my teaching style and throw my teaching philosophy out the window just because this was a slow class?

What should I do? Should I try to give in to my cooperating teacher's suggestions, or should I stick to what I believe I can make work? I have to make a decision right away. Which one should it be?

Questions

1. Based on your educational coursework, do you think that low achievers should be placed in ability groups? Explain.
2. Write a paragraph describing this situation from Mr. Gant's point of view. What, if anything, can you learn from looking at his perspective?
3. How important is coverage of information in teaching? Explain.
4. What role is played by teacher expectations in this case? In your own teaching?
5. What suggestions would you give Ralph for helping the cooperative learning groups function more smoothly?

CASE 21

Using the Internet: A Blessing or a Curse?

Nadine *Hallock runs into trouble with a student plagiarizing from the Internet. She wonders what the consequences should be and how to prevent this in the future.*

I knew the minute I started reading the paper that something was wrong. Kathleen was a good student, but this writing sounded, well, *professional*. I suspected right from the start that she couldn't have written it.

I have been student teaching at Greenfield Regional High School. Greenfield is a large school that draws students from all over the county. Most of the students are rather affluent, and the school has a reputation for having the highest SAT scores in the state.

I've been teaching a couple of different English classes, and Kathleen is a student in my 12th-grade honors class. This class is highly motivated, creative, and very competitive. Every day is exciting. We discuss books in depth, we debate our ideas passionately, and we share our own writing often.

Kathleen started off the semester very well. It didn't take me long to get to know her because she is outgoing and participates frequently in class discussions. Lately, however, her work has been uneven. She has missed a few minor assignments and has handed in most of her homework late.

When I asked her about this she said, "Oh, Ms. Hallock, I'm so sorry. I just started a new job at the bagel shop, and I'm having trouble finding the time to get my work done. But don't worry. I'm going to talk to the boss about changing my hours so I work more on the weekends. That will give me more time during the week for my assignments."

"How many hours are you working?" I asked.

"Only about 20 hours right now. It's not that much really," Kathleen responded.

"Aren't you also taking a couple of AP courses, Kathleen? Isn't this an awful lot to handle at the same time?"

"Nah, I'm sure I can manage it. I just need to get my schedule adjusted," Kathleen reassured me.

A month later, I noticed Kathleen was still behind on her work, and the end of the quarter was approaching. The students' major assignment was a term paper in which they needed to examine a theme from one of our readings. The students all met with me a few weeks before it was due to discuss their topics and research sources. Kathleen was doing a topic on *The Role of Fate versus the Control of Destiny in Shakespeare's King Lear.*

When Kathleen handed in her paper, right on time for a change, her topic was somewhat different than she had planned. Instead of her original topic she was now focusing on the role of the fool in *King Lear*. I wondered why she changed it. Then when I started reading the paper, my suspicions began. I just knew that Kathleen hadn't written it all. After a semester of reading my students' writing, I knew what to expect. I felt that I had a good understanding of their strengths and weaknesses. Kathleen just didn't write this well; there were too many sophisticated arguments, beautiful flowing prose, and many references.

I showed it to my cooperating teacher, Ms. Faison, and asked her what to do. She suggested I confront Kathleen right away and ask her about the work. Perhaps I could ask her how she came up with her ideas or where she got her resources. It sounded like a good strategy, and I agreed to speak with her the next day.

When I met with her I began, "Kathleen, I got a chance to read quickly through your paper. It looks very good. In fact I was wondering how you found the time to get all the resources for your work. Can you tell me how you put it all together?"

Kathleen cheerfully answered, "Oh, I spent a lot of time in the library getting ideas, and I also used the Internet to identify other things I wanted to read. It was a lot of work, but I'm pleased with how it came out."

"Did anyone help you with your work? It sounds a bit like you may have copied some of it," I probed.

"No, definitely not. I know you wanted us to work on our own for this assignment. All of that work is definitely my own," Kathleen answered a bit defensively.

"Well, I need to read it again and add my comments before I give it back to you," I added, confused about what else to say. I have to admit, she was very convincing, and it made me feel guilty for accusing her.

That evening, I was doing some of my own work on the Internet when I got an idea. I did a search for the title of Kathleen's paper. Much to my disappointment, I found the exact paper on a Web site. A college professor had published it as part of his resources for a college English course. Kathleen had not even bothered to change the title! I began to wonder if the other students have ever done this without me catching it. I could see how easy it was to do; it only took me a few minutes to find this paper.

Now I was angry. Not only did Kathleen copy the entire paper, but she had blatantly lied to me. I tried to think about all the pressure she was under and why she would resort to plagiarism when she is such a bright student. I felt this was an insult to me and the other students and had to be dealt with severely. First thing in the morning, I would speak with Ms. Faison. I knew she would be supportive, but I also knew that it was really my responsibility. I gave the assignment, and I was in charge of the class now. As much as I wanted to let Ms. Faison handle the whole problem, I knew I needed to take responsibility too.

What would I say to Kathleen? And what would be the appropriate consequences of such plagiarism? How would I prevent this in the future? I began to wonder if the Internet was more of a blessing or a curse!

Questions

1. What do you think the consequences of plagiarism should be in this case? Does your school have a policy on plagiarism?
2. Why do you think a student like Kathleen would plagiarize a paper in this way?
3. What exactly constitutes plagiarism? How would you define this for your students?
4. What suggestions do you have for preventing the abuse of information that is so readily available online while still being able to benefit from the Internet?
5. What problems, if any, have you seen in students' work schedules interfering with their academic work? How many hours of work do you think are appropriate? What time management strategies would you give your students?

CASE 22

Surfing Out of Control

Randy is pleased with his teaching of an advanced placement English class using computer-based instruction until he realizes that the students are spending most of their time surfing the Internet or playing games. He wonders how he can get them to pay attention and stay on task.

I felt like I had hit the jackpot when I was assigned to the Pollack School for the Gifted and Talented. First of all, I liked Pollack's location on a shady, live-oak covered block in an affluent area close to my home. Second, the school was known as one of the best high schools in the city, and I knew the students were really smart and probably wouldn't give me a hard time. The best part, though, was that I was put in Mr. Graham's advanced placement English class. This class was just so cool. I liked Mr. Graham right away, and he was a real role model. He was one of those popular teachers who could do no wrong. All the parents competed to get their kids in his classes, and the students loved him. In his class, there was a computer for every student, and most of the lessons were conducted on computers. This was good for me because I had taken a course in educational technology and have always been good with electronics. So I was excited to dive in.

At first, everything went OK. The students were polite, well dressed, and didn't act up at all. Sometimes, though, I would notice that they didn't seem to hear what I said. And a lot of times, their in-class work was superficial and lacking, compared to their formal essays, which were a lot better. I also noticed that the students mostly hunched over their computers, which were set up in rows facing the front of the room, but I assumed this was because they were working on the assignments I gave them.

As it turns out, I was clueless as to what was really going on in my class. I started to understand when one day, Jan Thompson, a young teacher like me, casually mentioned that when she walked by my door she noticed that a couple of my students were playing solitaire online while I was speaking. I was surprised, but things started to add up at that moment. No wonder I wasn't getting the quality of work that these college-bound seniors were capable of. I wasn't sure what to do, but I decided to walk around the room to check on what was going on.

What I did was walk out of the door to the room and then walk back in. That way the students couldn't see me because their backs were to the door. Doing this was a real eye opener for me. Sure enough, two students, probably the same ones Jan had seen earlier, were playing solitaire. And I noticed a few others checking their hotmail. But what really got me was that almost half of the class was surfing the net!

I immediately tried to get everyone's attention and told them there would be no surfing or games allowed. But even as I was speaking, I suspected that they were surfing. So I made them turn off their computers and repeated everything I had said. They seemed to listen, so I assumed that I had nipped this little problem in the bud. Wrong. The next day, I did the exact same thing, walked out of the room, walked back in. This time a couple of them were watching me, so I wasn't surprised to see their class work on the screen. But still, most of the class was bent over their screens surfing away.

That's when I really started to worry. Wasn't I teaching them anything? Was I a flop as a teacher? I had never seen Mr. Graham have this problem. He was like a magnet; anything he said got everyone's attention immediately. The class would notice even a raised eyebrow from him. So you can see why I wasn't comfortable talking to him about this problem. I considered just floating and not worrying, but I'm not that kind of guy. This was a problem I was determined to fix. Besides, my classroom and everything the students were doing in it were visible from the hall. The principal could just as easily see all this extracurricular activity going on while I tried to teach. I wanted more than anything else to be hired at Pollack. This was a plum assignment, and I didn't want to blow it. How could I get the students to stop surfing out of control?

Questions

1. Was the student teacher wrong in not discussing his problem with his cooperating teacher?
2. What room arrangement works best for computer classrooms?
3. What other alternatives might the student teacher have considered?

CASE 23

A Question of Motivation

Robert *has difficulty motivating his high school chemistry students. He wonders if he should be satisfied that they are polite and on-task, even though they seem to have no desire to learn more than they have to.*

Before I started my student teaching here at Thomas Jefferson High, I had heard the horror stories: "You'll never be able to get your class under control." "The teachers are old-fashioned." "The principal is demanding." "There's crime in that school; watch your back." None of these dire warnings proved to be true at all. From the first day I entered Jefferson, I never had the slightest concern about crime. Sure, Jefferson is in a poor neighborhood, but the halls were usually quiet and orderly—much more so, by the way, than my old high school in a much nicer part of town. What's more, the teachers were a dedicated group, the principal was very supportive of me, and when I taught my own chemistry lesson for the first time, the class sat politely with no one acting up. How good could it be?

Though if you asked me if there was a problem, I probably would have to say yes. I'm not sure if this was a real problem or just a cultural difference. I just moved to this southern city four years ago to go to the university and was always finding out—sometimes the hard way—that things were done differently here than they were on the East Coast where I grew up. But anyway, it was a problem for me. What I found was that I just couldn't get my class motivated. I'd assign a reading in the text, and then it would become clear to me that no one had done it. Or I'd have a test, and half the class would be out. And the half that was there wouldn't have studied. When we did an experiment, I'd explain patiently what they were supposed to do, but when I walked around the lab, I'd realize no one was doing it. I'd confront them, and they'd say they were doing it. I even called some of them in after school, but they didn't show up.

Of course, all this wasn't true for every single student. A few turned in their homework, showed up for the tests, did their experiments, and studied. But even with the better students, I noticed a real apathy about chemistry. They weren't curious at all. I knew that if they went to college they'd need to know this stuff. But they seemed to be halfhearted and only going through the motions.

I tried to talk with my class about their lack of motivation, but they just got evasive. I asked them what I could do to make the subject matter more interesting, and the response, though limited, was, "Everything's OK; What is the problem?" I really wanted them to be honest and to give me frank feedback. Usually, they just looked at me blankly as though they couldn't understand what I was saying—or didn't care. I threatened their grades, asked homework to be signed by their parents, even went around the room and demanded that each student say something, but nothing seemed to work. When I asked my cooperating teacher, Ms. Ali, about it, she sounded just like the students, saying, "Don't worry so much, Robert, everything is OK. Why upset the applecart?" I had wanted some honest feedback, but all she said was that I should consider myself lucky because some classes, especially the freshman ones, really acted up.

I wondered if I was making a mountain out of a molehill. Maybe I should have considered myself lucky that these students were so polite. Maybe it wasn't cool to act interested in school. Maybe they didn't want to go to college. Still, I had the sneaking suspicion that there was something they weren't saying. What could I do to motivate this group?

Questions

1. What would you have done in Robert's situation?
2. What alternative methods of teaching might have motivated students?
3. Do quiet students equate with learning students? Explain your answer.
4. Do you think the apathy that the student teacher faced is simply a question of "being cool"? Argue both sides of this question.
5. To what extent might disempowerment affect the students and their attitudes toward learning?

For Further Reading

Armstrong, T. (1987). *In their own way: Discovering and encouraging your child's personal learning style.* New York: Putnam.

> Having worked as a classroom teacher and a learning disabilities specialist, Armstrong is able to point out vividly the problems with labeling children. He left his position because he no longer believes in learning disabilities. This book shows us how to recognize the abilities rather than the disabilities in children. Although written for parents, it is very relevant to teachers as well.

Armstrong, T. (1994). *Multiple intelligences in the classroom.* Alexandria, VA: Association for Supervision and Curriculum Development.

> This book translates Gardner's theory into practical, accessible ideas for the classroom teacher. Through concrete examples, Armstrong helps the reader understand the powerful results of looking at intelligence in a broader way than is traditional.

Bredekamp, S., & Copple, C. (Eds.). (1997). *Developmentally appropriate practice in early childhood programs.* Washington, DC: National Association for the Education of Young Children.

> This book is the definitive source for information on the principles of developmentally appropriate practice and guidelines for making classroom decisions based on research and theory. It focuses on infants through eight-year-olds.

Freire, P. (1993). *Pedagogy of the oppressed.* New York: Continuum Publishing Company.

> Empowerment education ties education to actually bettering the position of the oppressed in society while educating humans from the culture of silence to critical thinking. Literacy is tied to empowerment.

Gardner, H. (1991). *The unschooled mind: How children think and how we should teach.* New York: Basic Books.

> Blending cognitive science and educational practice, Gardner shows how our schools work against the natural patterns of learning. He explains that teaching for understanding should be our main goal and shows why students are not learning what they should or not retaining what they have been taught.

Good, T. L., & Brophy, J. E. (2000). *Looking in classrooms.* (8th ed). New York: Longman.

> This is the definitive textbook for a comprehensive overview of the theory, research, and practice of effective classroom instruction.

Johnson, D. W., & Johnson, R. T. (1999). (5th ed.) *Learning together and alone: Cooperative, competitive, and individualistic learning.* Boston: Allyn & Bacon.

> This practical text integrates cooperative learning with competitive and individualistic learning by providing guidelines for managing critical issues such as teaching social skills, assessing competencies and involvement, and resolving conflict among group members. Besides describing each of these types of learning, the authors point out the pros and cons of each and review the relevant research needed to understand the value of each.

Kagan, S. (1994). *Cooperative learning.* San Clemente, CA: Author.

This book is a practical guide to cooperative learning theory, methods, and lesson designs. It is a thorough resource for applying cooperative learning to all ages, from kindergarten through adult.

Slavin, R. (1990). *Cooperative learning.* Upper Saddle River, NJ: Prentice Hall.

This book comprehensively explains the rationale and research behind cooperative learning, with an overview of many different proven methods and resources.

Vygotsky, L. (1978). *Mind in society: The development of higher psychological processes.* Cambridge, MA: Harvard University Press.

This theory of development shows how social experiences enable the internalization of higher thought processes. It introduces the concept of the zone of proximal development and the role of scaffolding in helping learners reach new levels of development.

SECTION 3

Challenges of Diversity

CASE 24

Who Will My Girls Be?

Elizabeth Anton questions what happens to girls' identities when they are mixed into a predominantly male kindergarten class. She struggles as a student teacher to reflect on the ways in which girls and boys are being stereotyped and shortchanged.

I am teaching in an all-day kindergarten consisting of 21 children: 16 boys and 5 girls in a small parochial school. There is only one kindergarten class in the school, as there is only one of every grade.

My name is Elizabeth. I am doing my student teaching in this school, and I am also employed as the regular classroom teacher. Therefore, I am alone in the classroom, with a mentor for advice but no cooperating teacher. This, of course, offers both advantages and disadvantages. I can make mistakes without the watchful eye of another teacher, and I have freedom to teach in my own way. On the other hand, I lack the guidance and support of a full-time cooperating teacher.

During arrival, the children seem to have their routine down pretty well. The students turn in homework pads from the night before and have folders ready to be checked to see if there are any notes from home. As I do the attendance slip, I am reminded each day of the lopsided enrollment in my classroom.

This bothers me somewhat. The first news I received about my class was that it was almost all boys. I am worried that the girls do not receive enough attention. Am I constantly calling on the boys for the answers? Why do I say, "OK, *boys* and girls, let's turn to page 22 . . .?" Do I always put boys first in my room? I spend a lot of time wondering if my girls think that I am not fair to them. I am concerned about the seating arrangement: should I have seated the girls at one table? I thought that way they might alienate themselves from the boys altogether. Instead, I spread them out with one girl at each table. Was that a wise decision?

We have decided that responsibility is a big part of having a well-run classroom. We change jobs every week, with a boy helper and a girl helper each week. But I don't have enough girls to go around. It seems the boys always have the jobs; and if I try to give three girls jobs every week, it's not fair to the boys. The boys have to wait so long for their turn to have a job.

This problem also showed up when we put on a little skit for Thanksgiving. All of the children dressed up as Native Americans, with their paper bag (animal hide) vests and feather headdresses. Should I have made the girls be little pilgrim girls? Do they get lost in the crowd of Indians? I wonder. . . .

I realize that reflection is a big part of effective teaching. I honestly try to reflect at the end of each day, thinking about what I've done, what I've said, and how I've said it. I try not to have favorites, but it's so hard. I try not to judge or label students, but that's just as hard. When you only have a handful of girls in a sea of boys, it becomes even harder not to label them; I know who is the "responsible" one, the "lazy" one, the "quiet" one. It's not as easy to label the boys because they surprise me from time to time. Sometimes they're quiet; sometimes they're not. Sometimes they're just "wild boys." Oops! There I go again, thinking that same thought: boys will be boys. . . . Who will my girls be?

Questions

1. How do you feel about the description of Elizabeth's classroom and activities? What things might influence the students' feelings about gender?
2. What advice would you give Elizabeth about dealing with her small percentage of girls? Do you agree with how she has handled things in her class? Why or why not?
3. What other strategies for combating gender bias can you come up with? Try to brainstorm as many possibilities as you can.
4. Is it important for classes to be gender balanced? Is having so few girls a problem? How would your answer change if the class were fifth grade? Eighth grade? High school? Does your reasoning hold true for race or social class as well?
5. Are there other issues in this case besides the stated problem with gender bias? What other issues can you identify?

CASE 25

White Faces Don't Want to Be My Friend

Laryn Coulter, a student teacher in elementary health education, has difficulty managing one of her first-grade classes, primarily because Jasmine constantly puts her to the test. After trying out many classroom management strategies, she finally develops an effective approach and gets Jasmine to open up in discussions—only to have her bring up racial issues that make Laryn unsure of what to do.

When September rolled around—all too fast for me—I started my student teaching assignment with much anxiety but also with a real need to prove that I could do this. I was assigned primary grades one through five in the area of health education. The school is located in a rural town that is small but culturally diverse.

Health in my school is considered a special area of learning. This means that all students receive health education only once every six days for a 50-minute period. Each class consists of approximately 25 students, so I see a couple of hundred students each week. This creates a definite classroom management problem: students need time to know me. They need to learn my rules and how I will enforce them. More important, I need to know each child. I need to know whether a particular day's behavior is typical or the result of something unknown to me. All of this takes time, and time, I discovered, was not something I had much of.

The importance of knowing what is behind children's behaviors instead of just attempting to control them was brought home to me by one of my students, a first grader named Jasmine. I sensed almost immediately that Jasmine was going to be a challenge. During my first observation class, I noted her disruptive behavior. Still, I had to be fair. Could this be an unusual day for her? Were there issues I was unaware of? I didn't want to let first impressions prejudice my judgment, but I noted that Jasmine talked throughout the whole class, several times got out of her seat without permission, and often did not even attempt her seatwork. I learned that she also made frequent trips to the nurse's office with vague and minor physical complaints.

I decided to observe how my cooperating teacher, Ms. Michaels, dealt with Jasmine. Ms. Michaels is experienced, kind, and firm. Who better to learn from? So when Jasmine acted up in the second class I observed, I noticed that my cooperating teacher's strategies ranged from ignoring her behavior to firm, clear disapproval. I was impressed that Ms. Michaels never lost her cool.

When I began teaching, I clearly stated, "Even though I am going to be taking over teaching the class, all of Ms. Michaels's classroom rules will stay the same." But I was a new teacher. I would have to be tested, and who better to test me than

Jasmine? She immediately stepped up her talking to anyone who would listen. She squirmed and faced different directions in the class. She rocked on her chair. She played with objects in her desk. She wandered through the classroom. When it came time for seatwork, she accomplished next to nothing. I also noted that Jasmine had no friends, no one to connect with among her peers.

My first strategy was to give gentle guidance back to more desirable behavior. I gave positive affirmation to students who worked quietly. I praised all completed work. I made examples of student work; as long as students made an attempt to carry out the assignment, I gave them stars. But Jasmine's behavior did not improve. Modeling just would not work, at least with her.

Next I decided to ignore Jasmine's behavior. I was spending far too much time commenting on it, I thought. It was not fair to the other students. I hoped that, given no reinforcement, this behavior would minimize or disappear. Yet I was sadly mistaken. Jasmine's behavior actually became worse. She displayed anger, stomping her feet, slamming down her books, emitting loud noises, and fighting with other students.

Maybe Jasmine needed attention, I reasoned. I began to feel sorry for her. I believe that children want to be good, and I know that Jasmine did not want to be yelled at. But it was difficult because I did not want to reinforce bad behavior. I started to speak briefly with Jasmine when she was quiet and to look for areas of interest that I could use to draw her into the lessons. Still, there were no obvious changes.

Then a breakthrough occurred when I least expected it. As part of a dental unit, I was reading the class a book about a missing tooth. The book told about two best friends who were always alike until one of them lost a tooth and the other experienced profound disappointment over being different. As I led the class in a discussion about how people did not have to be the same to be friends, I was struck by the fact that Jasmine was leaning forward and listening intently. I saw her slowly raise her hand and hesitantly begin to speak. She said, "I get upset because I have a black face, and white faces don't want to be my friend."

The students were suddenly quiet. I stood there in front of the class, looking at Jasmine's upturned face gazing expectantly at me and at the faces of her classmates staring at her. I was unsure of what to do. I said to myself, "Oh, no, I don't want to comment on this." I thought, "I am too new to deal with racial issues." I sensed that this was a crucial moment not only for Jasmine but also for me as a teacher. I just didn't know what to say next.

Questions

1. What advice would you give Laryn in this situation? What should she say or do? Based on your understanding of the development of social skills, self-concept, and perspective-taking in young children, what do you think Laryn can do in the long term to meet the needs of all of her students?
2. Should student teachers deal with racial issues? Explain.

3. Brainstorm ways in which teachers can promote racial understanding and acceptance of differences.
4. How has your view of Jasmine's behavior changed, if at all, knowing the information about her feelings that she shared?
5. Why do you think the student teacher's efforts at controlling Jasmine's behavior were unsuccessful? Think about what you have learned or are learning in your education courses. What do you think she could do instead?

CASE 26

Two Dads

Kathleen McCall wonders how to restore the self-esteem of a third grader who is being teased because he has told the class that he has two dads. How can she enable the other students to be more understanding?

I sat in my classroom during lunch thinking about my student teaching. In September, when I began my student teaching at the Mercer School, a public school in the center of a medium-sized city, I noticed that the makeup of my third-grade class was very diverse. Ms. Heilbroner, my cooperating teacher, set an example by treating diversity as something positive.

I admired Ms. Heilbroner's lessons, which focused on the individuality of each child. For example, one lesson that she taught required that students interview someone from their block about the music they liked, the food they ate, and their lives as young people. In this multicultural community, that meant hearing about Indian, Arab, African-American, Ecuadorian, Salvadoran, and Polish cultures, to name just a few. The children obviously loved sharing their interviews, which they eventually included in a newspaper about the blocks that made up their city. I observed closely the way in which Ms. Heilbroner validated all of the contributions. I vowed to follow my cooperating teacher's lead in my own facilitation of this class.

When it was finally time for me to begin to teach, I was elated. This was a dream come true. I shared many valuable lessons with my students that were very successful. Ms. Heilbroner commended me on my efforts. "You already teach like someone with years of experience," she said. This compliment thrilled me. I knew my internship was developing into a strong learning experience that would definitely prepare me for my chosen profession. The students seemed genuinely excited about my lessons, and there was a growing sense of community in the classroom.

That is, until about two weeks ago. One of my main themes focused on the family and the many characteristics that make up each one. During a class discussion dealing with parents, one of my students, Mark, mentioned that he did not have a mom. "I have two dads," he explained. This comment was met with an eerie silence and then a few giggles. Not sure what to say, I smiled and asked Mark if he would care to talk about his family with the rest of the class. Seeing his peers' reaction to his comment, Mark shook his head no. I went on to the other students very casually but kept the incident in the back of my mind for the rest of the day.

In the days that followed, I began to realize that the other students in the class were taunting Mark. "You have two dads," I heard them chant. "You have two dads." And once even, "Mark is gay." At one point, I felt compelled to speak firmly to a few of the students who were making the taunts. But the teasing nevertheless continued.

The teasing has also had a serious impact on Mark. He has always been considered a bright, well-rounded child. In the past, he has worked well with his friends and has been popular with the other children. He also has shared with Ms. Heilbroner and me his future dreams of college and career as a veterinarian.

Since that fateful day, however, Mark has become withdrawn and almost angry. He now sits in the back of the room alone and barely finishes his assignments. His grades are beginning to slip, which is very unlike him. When I tried to speak to him yesterday, he simply stood in the room and did not say a word, which was upsetting for both of us. When I related the whole incident to Ms. Heilbroner, I was surprised that she had no easy answers.

Now, sitting at my desk alone, I am beginning to question my actions. Why did the students react the way they did? I always thought that this class was very close and that members shared their problems together. Could I have reacted the wrong way when Mark mentioned his family lifestyle? What can I do to help this child? How can I help the rest of the class understand his situation?

Questions

1. Write about this dilemma from Mark's point of view. What can you learn about your role as a classroom facilitator from seeing the situation through his eyes?
2. What if Mark had not told the class about his family? Would this situation have been better? Was it important for him to be able to share this?
3. Do you believe that students' private lives should be discussed in classrooms? Why? Why not?
4. Brainstorm ways in which Kathleen could promote appreciation of nontraditional families among her students. What suggestions do you have for her to deal with the taunting? Have you experienced or observed this kind of teasing in your class? What have you seen teachers do to help such a situation?
5. What role should Mark's family play in deciding how to handle this situation and what information should be shared? Should Kathleen speak to family members about Mark?

CASE 27

What to Do About Gender Equity?

Louise Patel, a student teacher committed to gender equity, becomes disturbed that only females have been chosen to participate in a fifth-grade cooking class.

One morning during my internship, I found myself at the fifth-grade teachers' meeting. I was so excited that they had included me. I had been student teaching in Ms. Carmichael's class since September, and things had been going really well. Ms. Carmichael had taken extra care to include me in every aspect of teaching, inviting me to conferences with parents, introducing me to the other teachers, and treating me as an equal. I was grateful that I had such an understanding, caring, cooperating teacher.

Let me give you some background. I am a social studies major and chose this school, P.S. 320, because of its excellent reputation and student-centered philosophy. I had heard too many horror stories of progressive student teachers who ended up having to teach from the text or from worksheets, so I took the bull by the horns and requested a school that I knew was nontraditional and forward thinking.

I actually fell in love with this school the first time I visited. The walls of the sparkling clean halls were adorned with brightly colored artwork, photographs of African-American and Hispanic leaders, and quotes about how everyone can succeed. Classroom doors seemed to compete, each one with student work more beautiful than the other. Floating out of all the classes was the low, busy buzz of students talking in groups and activity centers. I was in utopia!

From day one, I was awed by the faculty. Not only did they have the student-centered philosophy that I had learned in my teacher education courses, but they had absolutely great teaching ideas. Plus they were experienced in promoting a multicultural curriculum. This was something that they practiced every single day, not just on ethnic holidays. I was going to learn a lot from this group of highly dedicated teachers.

It was Ms. Carmichael's idea that I come to the teachers' meeting. She said that relating to the other faculty was an important part of the job. I was a little bit nervous but happy to be included. Anyway, I was sitting there minding my own business and taking in everything. I knew this was going to be a great learning experience for me. All was well until the topic of picking which students would be allowed to participate in cooking came up.

You see, each year a group of students is selected across the three fifth grades to cook. It's really a great idea. This group cooks a dinner based on an ethnic theme under the supervision of one of the teachers and parent volunteers. Then the food is served to a party of all the students in the fifth-grade classes. The teachers believe that by tasting the foods of the many cultures that make up this school, the children will learn respect for diversity. The teachers' meeting that I was attending was called to plan the event and to pick the children who would participate.

Finally the time came for the teachers to discuss how they were going to go about the selection of the students. After some discussion, they decided that the best thing to do would be to choose a few exemplary students from each class. Of course, those who were well behaved were chosen, but what bothered me was that every one of those teachers happened to choose female students to cook! I was quite annoyed to say the least. I understood that for the most part, the girls were easier to work with, but didn't the teachers realize the message they were sending to the other students?

I was surprised that the teachers at this of all schools would choose only girls for the cooking class. These were teachers who were well-known for their liberal views and accomplishments. I knew that they believed in gender equity; I had even heard them talk about it. But they didn't even seem to notice that they had chosen an all-girl cooking group.

My parents taught me to stand up for what I think is right. They always made a point of trying to treat me and my brother as equals and raised me to demand equality. I am a member of a women's organization on campus, where I am known for being outspoken on issues of gender. I feel strongly that women can do anything that men can. And I certainly don't want to be the kind of teacher who furthers stereotypes.

Still, I didn't know what to do. After all, I was only a student myself. Should I say something and risk offending Ms. Carmichael, who would be evaluating me? Or should I keep my mouth shut and allow this to happen? I was completely torn. I was so angry that I did not even know if I could say something without exploding. I was not sure if it even was my place to say something. I was a guest. These were their students, not mine. What should I do?

Questions

1. What are Louise's options in this case? What would you do? Why?
2. If you had to select a group of students to participate in a special activity, what criteria would you use to make your choice? Why?
3. What happens when good behavior is consistently used to determine who gets to participate in enrichment activities? What does that do to students who aren't considered good? What does it do to students who are?
4. What should a teacher do if the females resist the inclusion of males as cooks or if the males refuse to participate in "women's work"?
5. What classroom tasks did males take on in your educational past? Females? What messages did that division of labor, if there was one, carry?

CASE 28

Am I Going to Die?

***Margaret** Dawson ponders how to deal with her fifth-grade students, who are teasing a child with cancer who has lost her hair.*

It was September, and the fall was off to a great start. In just one week, I would be beginning my student teaching. I would be teaching in an elementary school in my own neighborhood in the urban area where I live. I was relieved that I had gotten this assignment instead of one at a suburban school because I am familiar with urban children and their needs. After all, I was one myself. So what could go wrong?

I was very excited about reporting for the first day of my internship at P.S. 188. As I neared the tall, soot-covered brick building with bars over the windows, I thought to myself how glad I was to be here. Nevertheless, I also feared that my students would not like me, would not find me funny, or would not learn from me. I honestly did not know what I would do.

Well, I soon found myself in room 14, and everything seemed fine. This was definitely a cheerful learning environment. My cooperating teacher was Ms. Brown. She was a small, dark, vivacious woman with flashing eyes, wearing bright red lipstick. The children obviously loved her. I admired her teaching style and especially her ability to actively listen to each child. Ms. Brown told me that just as soon as I felt comfortable, she would turn everything over to me. I was a little scared but appreciated her willingness to let me get the experience I needed. After all, I had heard about student teachers who had a problem getting to actually teach.

Most of the children in this fifth grade were 10 years old. They all looked like your average, urban elementary school children. Each one of them really seemed enthusiastic about starting the new school year. I began by going around the room and assisting the students as Ms. Brown taught her lessons. I enjoyed answering the children's questions and helping them with their work. Soon I had a good relationship with them and actually looked forward to the time when I could take over the lessons.

Well, it didn't take long. Before I knew it, I was trying out all my good ideas from the past three years at college. I was attempting to create a strong community, and the students seemed interested in my lessons, which I had designed to make learning fun and meaningful at the same time. I was really on cloud nine, looking at their eager faces.

This is where Stacy comes in. Stacy wasn't, I guess you could say, a normal 10-year-old girl. She would have been like any other girl, except for one thing. Stacy didn't have any hair. She was completely bald. I know, through my mom who knows her aunt, that she has leukemia. The other children do not know that, though. I guess the other kids simply think she was born without any hair.

When I took over the class, it didn't seem to me that Stacy was having any problems in particular. I did notice that the other children seemed to shy away from her, but there was no sign of anything being seriously wrong in her relationship with them. Mostly she did her work and sat quietly when she finished without too much interaction with the other children. She seemed not to want to be in the spotlight.

Stacy did not usually wear a wig. However, on the day she did choose to wear a wig, there were whispers going around as soon as the other students saw her. All I heard was, "Stacy has a wig on," and, "Look at Stacy." The wig was obvious to everyone because she looked so different in it.

It was also clear that Stacy felt uncomfortable with this sudden attention. All day long, I was faced with questions from the children: "How did Stacy all of a sudden grow hair?" "Why does Stacy look funny?" How could I answer those questions? I felt that she wore the wig because the other girls were always braiding and brushing one another's hair and perhaps she felt left out.

In the days that followed, none of the other children made fun of Stacy on a regular basis—actually not until they got into arguments with her. When they argued, they would call her baldy. The taunts broke my heart, and, as Stacy's tears showed, it was obvious that they broke her heart, too. I searched my mind about what I could do. In frustration, I yelled at the others for their name-calling. The children stared at me in surprise. Even though I had vowed to myself never to raise my voice in the classroom, I evidently made some sort of impression on the students by doing just that.

So far, so good. Everything was under control. Well, that is what I thought. I thought I had this Stacy situation taken care of. But one morning, at the end of October, I saw Stacy all alone and crying. I approached her to see if I could comfort her tears. She then told me that two of the girls were saying that she was going to die. I was horrified. This had gone entirely too far.

Now what was I to do? What could I possibly say to this 10-year-old girl who was crying in my arms? Could any of my words comfort her? How do you explain to children why a student loses his or her hair? Is it appropriate for me to explain or talk about her illness? Would that just make Stacy feel worse? Should I treat this sick child differently? My questions concerning what to do about Stacy are endless.

Questions

1. What, if anything, might Margaret have done ahead of time to help Stacy feel accepted in this classroom? What should she do now?
2. Do you think it is appropriate to talk about Stacy's illness? Brainstorm strategies for helping the other children understand the illness.
3. Is teasing and name calling just a part of childhood or can we get children to be more empathic? What evidence can you cite to back up your position?
4. Should special children like Stacy be treated differently from other children? Explain. Try to interview someone in this position to see what his or her perspective is.
5. What should the role of Stacy's parents be in deciding what action to take in this situation?

CASE 29

Should We Celebrate Holidays?

Megan Loughlin is looking forward to the fall holidays, preparing many theme-related activities and celebrations for her seventh-grade English class, when she discovers that some of the children in her class do not celebrate Halloween. Just when she thinks she has come up with a solution to this dilemma, she realizes it is more complicated than she thought.

As I began my student teaching experience, I found myself looking for pumpkin patterns, crossword puzzles with witches, and poems about turkeys. I thought that in order to become a successful teacher, I needed to get my students interested by having them write about details associated with the more popular holidays. Boy, I was dead wrong!

At first my assumptions were affirmed. When my cooperating teacher told the students we were going to make marbleized pumpkins and write scary stories about Halloween, I figured that this was going to be exciting and a great learning experience for me. What I did not anticipate was how many students would refuse to participate in these supposedly fun and exciting activities.

One morning I asked the students to get out their homework, which included a first draft of the scary Halloween story they were to write. I was surprised when some of the students hadn't even begun yet. Michael, a very self-assured young man, finally raised his hand to explain, "Miss Loughlin, we don't celebrate Halloween or any other holidays in my family, and my parents don't let me write about things like this." Two of the other students quickly agreed with him, explaining that they were Jehovah's Witnesses. Two more students told me that they were Christians who just didn't celebrate Halloween. I felt a cold rush come upon me. What was I going to do? What would I use to decorate my classroom? What kind of stories could I have them write about? Most of all, I thought, what was I going to do about Christmas and the holidays that were so important to me?

I realized I needed time to think this all out, so I told the kids we would discuss this later and come up with a solution. I went home that night a little depressed and very confused. I needed to reevaluate myself and my style of teaching. How was I going to turn this into a positive experience? How was I going to prevent these students from feeling excluded or believing that they had done something wrong? Most of all, how was I going to respect all of my students and their cultures?

First, I decided to do a little research. I went to the library and got information about several of the religious customs of the students in my class so that at least I had a rough idea of what they did and did not believe and recognize. Then I decided to ask each of the five students if they wanted to tell me more about their traditions and beliefs or not. Four of the students seemed very excited and were more than willing to share information with me. Marissa, the fifth student, quietly asked, "Would it be okay if I just write about it? Maybe I could get my mother to write some information for you, too." I felt reassured and said, "Of course! I look forward to it." The next day I received a note from Marissa and her mother explaining some of their cultural and religious traditions. Her mother added a nice note saying that she understood the situation and my concern.

Now that I had all the information I needed, what was I going to do about class activities? Should I stop doing projects concerning holidays? Should I include projects with all kinds of holidays? I was now more educated about religions but not about what to do in the classroom.

By now it was the middle of October and we had not done any more art projects or stories concerning Halloween. I decided to assign a book to read about Pocahontas and to explore the concept of culture. All of the students have written a story about their own culture and have included the music they listen to, the food they eat, and so on. This worked out very well. They not only enjoy writing about themselves but also love the projects we did in conjunction with the culture study: making masks, baking ethnic food, and decorating the classroom with cultural artifacts. If you were to walk into the classroom right now, you would find Native American headdresses and masks, personal stories about cultures, Cuban coffee, but most of all no ghosts, witches, or pumpkins.

I had all but convinced myself that there is no need for all of the hype related to holidays and the decorations and stories. I really thought that even though we were not planning to celebrate any holidays, the class was flowing smoothly and not missing anything. Then this morning, I overheard some students who were getting books from their lockers, "I can't believe we don't get to celebrate Halloween or any other holidays anymore. Just because of those weirdoes in our class who don't celebrate holidays. That really stinks." Another student added, "Yeah, it's like the holidays we celebrate don't matter. How fair is that?"

I felt my heart sink. I hadn't realized they felt like that at all! Had I offended some students at the expense of others? How could I meet everyone's need to have their traditions affirmed? What was I going to do now?

Questions

1. Does your school have a formal policy on celebrating holidays? Do you think there should be one? If so, what should that policy be?
2. What advice would you give Megan about her dilemma? What do you think about her approach to holidays and affirming culture? What could she do differently?
3. How important do you think it is to have multicultural education? Do you think that you can have an effective multicultural curriculum when your class is racially and culturally homogeneous?
4. Have you ever felt different from the majority in school or in other social situations? In what ways do your personal experiences determine how you analyze this case?

5. Do you think that religion should be part of the school curriculum? Why? Why not? If you answered yes, explain how the curriculum should be structured. What should be included? How should it be taught? Do your state curriculum standards contain religion as part of the curriculum?

CASE 30

Struggling with Learning Disabilities

Jim Parker, assured by his cooperating teacher that his own learning disabilities would create no problem, is overwhelmed by his need to help two learning disabled students in the eighth-grade class where he is student teaching.

I'd been looking forward to student teaching since I returned to school two years ago. The district in which I was placed is close to the suburban community where I live, which was convenient. My excitement grew as summer faded away and September approached. On my first day in this eighth-grade classroom, Miss Suarez, my cooperating teacher, and I briefly discussed what my responsibilities would be. At this time I revealed that I had a learning disability so that we could discuss how this might affect my teaching. Miss Suarez assured me there would be no problem, which at first relieved me.

As the week passed, though, I began to worry. I noticed many inconsistencies in Miss Suarez's classroom management, especially when dealing with learning disabled students. Joe, who is new to the district, was a student with whom I personally identified. He was having difficulty with assignments and keeping focused. I worked well with Joe, and he seemed to respond to my attention. Nevertheless, his attention span was short, and he had a hard time remaining still. I wanted to do everything I could to help him because I remembered so vividly how it felt to be in his position.

Miss Suarez finally contacted Joe's former junior high school. His previous teacher informed us that Joe had been prohibited from attending school field trips and forbidden from participating in extracurricular activities. He had also not been permitted to sit among his peers because of his behavior problems. Immediately following our conversation with his former teacher, my cooperating teacher returned to the classroom, where I was proctoring a test. Despite the fact that Joe was behaving and obediently answering questions, my cooperating teacher publicly commanded him to collect his supplies and move his desk next to hers. Joe never got a second chance. I felt as if she had punished me, too.

Another student I am concerned about is Melissa. She is a very shy and extremely conscientious girl who goes to the resource room for reading problems. One unfortunate day, Melissa forgot to have a parent sign her test, which is our required classroom procedure. Although Melissa regularly earned good grades and had never been reprimanded in class, my cooperating teacher scolded her aloud and then punished her. Melissa sat at her desk with tears beginning to stream down her face.

"Melissa, please come up here," Miss Suarez ordered. Melissa dutifully approached the desk. "Melissa, can I see your student planner?" Melissa, still crying, retrieved her planner for the teacher. After looking through it, the teacher said, "See here. It says to get tests signed. I'm sorry, Melissa. It's your own fault." I wanted to comfort her or at least offer her a tissue.

Every time something like this happens, I cringe. I remember only too well my own feelings struggling with a learning disability in school. My dilemma is simply this: I am supposed to be an advocate for children, yet I am also supposed to support my cooperating teacher. After all, I am a guest in this school. I don't know how healthy it is for me or the students to feel so personally involved in their problems. I am worried that I cannot be impartial or objective when it comes to students with learning disabilities. On the other hand, maybe I don't need to be so objective. Maybe what would help these students the most is to have someone really understand what they are going through.

Questions

1. Do you think that it is necessary to be objective and impartial when you're teaching? Why or why not? Is it possible to be too involved in your students' problems?
2. What do you think Miss Suarez's view of this case is? Compare her perspective to Jim's. How can looking at both sides help you understand this case better?
3. Do you have experience with learning disabled children in your class? How have you felt personally in working with them? What do you think they need most to be successful in your class? Try to interview a learning disabled student or adult to get his or her perspective.
4. What options does Jim have in this case? What do you think he can do that is in the best interest of the students? How can he specifically help Joe and Melissa? What have you learned in your educational coursework that sheds light on the public humiliation these students experienced? What other courses of action could have been taken?
5. Do you agree that Jim's learning disability will not affect his teaching? What might he have to do to compensate?

CASE 31

Are You Gay?

John Rittling begins his student teaching in a high school English class. His worst fears come true when a disruptive student asks him the one question he has been dreading.

The class was silent, with everyone, including Ms. Phillips, my cooperating teacher, looking at me. In a malicious voice, Cheryl repeated her question, laughing, "Mr. Rittling, are you gay?" I noticed a few of the students catch one another's eyes, also laughing, and then again it was deadly quiet as 27 expectant faces awaited my reply.

I had been student teaching at Longview for only a week before I heard these dreaded words come out of Cheryl's mouth. I had feared someone would make a remark or question my sexual orientation, but I was totally unprepared for it when it happened. What could I say or do?

Actually, my student teaching had started out fairly smoothly. Longview is an established yellow-brick urban school in a town adjacent to the one I have spent all but the first three years of my life in. I would like to get a job in a school like this, especially since I don't have a car and can't travel far from my home. I know that there are openings here, and I have been told that male teachers are much in demand in this district.

Ms. Phillips, my cooperating teacher, is really wonderful. She treats me like a peer, leaving the lessons up to me. She even told me not to worry about making mistakes because student teaching is a time to try things out and to learn and that no one learns without making mistakes. To tell you the truth, with this kind of support, I felt totally confident and able to handle my classes well, which I have. I am proud of my lessons and was looking forward to a great internship.

Longview is truly an excellent environment for a student teacher. The rest of the faculty here has been friendly from the day I began, and I am truly amazed that most of the students seem to listen to me and call me Mr. Rittling instead of Johnny as I'm known at home and back at the college. It's a great feeling to be a teacher. By and large, the students at this school seem to take learning seriously and to respect their teachers—that is, except for Cheryl.

Left back twice, Cheryl is older and wiser than the other 10th graders and has a big mouth. She really gets my goat. If I ask the class to read a passage in the text, she complains loudly that it is too hard. When I pass out worksheets, she mutters that the exercise is Mickey Mouse. She never does her homework and always insists that she doesn't have to listen to me. In fact, any time I stand before the class to talk, she puts her head down on the desk and makes loud snoring sounds, causing her peers to laugh. Cheryl has a chip on her shoulder and seems to especially have it in for me.

It was on the second day of my student teaching that I noticed that Cheryl was making thinly veiled hints about my sexuality, stopping short, however, of outright questioning it. For example, when I was giving a writing assignment on colors, she proclaimed to the class that she would expect my favorite to be pink. "Watch out, boys!" she warned, the expression in her eyes almost daring me to say something. I just ignored her, and the other students did, too, but it bothered me that she said this. Then a couple of days later, she called another student a homophobic name, staring pointedly at me as she did. Again I pretended not to hear her, and things went on as normal.

Yesterday after school, Ms. Phillips warned me not to take anything Cheryl said too personally. "She's had a rough life," my cooperating teacher explained, pointing out that Cheryl sometimes disrupts her teaching, too. While I was grateful for this show of support from Ms. Phillips, it certainly did not help me know how to respond to Cheryl. I can't tell my cooperating teacher that I'm gay because I think I wouldn't be able to get a job anywhere in this district if the word got out. Besides, whose business is my sexuality? Certainly, no one else really talks about theirs. Yet on the other hand, I hate to remain silent. I worry about what that says to gay students in the class. I remember how suffocating the silence was when I was a student. This issue definitely wasn't addressed in my education classes. But I have to respond somehow. I feel that Cheryl is escalating her comments as time goes by. What on earth should I do?

Questions

1. How do you think John should respond to Cheryl's remarks? Have you ever been made uncomfortable by a student's remark or questions? How did you respond? To what extent should a teacher's life be private? How much should you share with students?
2. Should sexual orientation be discussed in school? If so, in what ways? Should it be a part of the curriculum? How do the teachers feel about this issue at your school? The parents?
3. What do you know about adolescent development, specifically psychosocial development, that can help you better understand this case and possible solutions? How can Erikson's theory enlighten this discussion? In what other ways do students suffer from being different from the mainstream?
4. Do you think John should tell his cooperating teacher that he is gay? Why? Why not? Should he tell the students? How do you feel about John's need to help other gay students not suffer the "suffocating silence"?
5. What do you think Ms. Phillips's perspective is on this case? Retell this case through her eyes. In what ways does taking her perspective help you find other possible interpretations and solutions?

CASE 32

Them and Us

Ann *Ricardo is dismayed to learn that there is a racial issue behind the isolation of a group of newcomers from other students in her suburban high school class.*

I began my student teaching in a suburban high school that has a reputation of being one of the best in the area. The school, housed in a spacious, modern building, was renowned for its sophisticated computer labs and other high-tech equipment as well as its strong teaching staff and bright, motivated student body.

I had looked forward to teaching for a long time, and at last the moment had arrived. I was pleasantly surprised to find that this was a job that I could do well. During my first week at the school, however, I realized that I was facing a problem. I noticed that some of the students were isolating themselves from the rest of the class.

I first noticed that three of the students—Carmen, Mayra, and Lucy—sat together in a tight little bunch for every class. I neither heard these group members speak to other students nor heard other students speak to them. The class environment was made up of six round tables, each with six chairs. This setting was aimed at facilitating group interaction, and usually the group work seemed to go smoothly. But I was worried about what was happening with the group of three. When I called their separation to the attention of my cooperating teacher, Ms. Jones simply stated that the three were new to the school this semester.

While reflecting on this situation at home, I came up with what I hoped was a solution. The next day, I discussed with Ms. Jones the plan I had mapped out to try to encourage the three students to sit with the others. "When the fourth-period algebra class meets, I would like to have the chairs around five of the six tables," I said. "That way, they'll have to sit with the other students in the class." Ms. Jones concurred that this could be a good way to get the three young women to interact with the rest of the class.

All morning long, I looked forward to this class to see what would happen. When the moment arrived, the tables were set up as planned. As the students filed into the class, they took seats without comment about the changed arrangement. The three newcomers, however, gathered together, then took chairs from the other tables and proceeded to sit at the sixth table, the three of them alone.

My spirits dropped as I gazed at the three, whispering together, their heads almost touching. How could I get them to interact with the others? Why were they so shy? This was my first real problem as a student teacher, and I had no idea how to solve it.

After class, I commented to Ms. Jones, "Did you see how they went out of their way to sit alone again, even after having had no chairs at the one table? I really don't know what to do now to break up this bunch."

"They do seem determined not to sit with the other students," Ms. Jones commented. After a moment's thought, she added, "Tomorrow during class, we can try one of the exercises I have in mind. It will have them separate, and each one will go to a different table to be seated with the other students."

I thought to myself, "This will be a challenge."

The next day, the students arrived for their algebra class, and the three girls again chose to sit together without so much as a nod at anyone else. Ms. Jones began giving out worksheets and instructions for completing them. The students were advised that as a group at each table, they should work together on the sheets and be sure everyone in the group understood the problems. Each table was given a different set of problems to work on. When the students were finished with the worksheets, Ms. Jones advised them that they would go to different tables now and be the experts on the worksheets that they had completed.

The three students that had not separated in prior classes were now going to be separated and have to interact with the other students in the class. Looks of concern came over their faces. I reinforced Ms. Jones's instructions and advised them that they were to teach the other students what they had learned from their worksheet. They were going to be the experts, the teachers. The students followed the directions reluctantly. I noticed that Carmen kept looking at Ms. Jones with an appeal in her eyes.

Once the experts began sharing, I saw that the other students were not listening to the three girls. All three had sullen expressions on their faces and seemed to make their contributions as brief as possible, especially compared to the contributions of the others in the class. I knew that the problem was not solved.

After class, I was not surprised to see that the three students remained to speak with me. After a moment's awkward silence, Carmen began, "We don't like to go to different tables. It makes us uncomfortable. We want to stay together." At this, Mayra and Lucy vigorously nodded.

I responded, "But if you stay at the same table, you're not going to get to know the other students in the class."

"The other students here don't want us in this school," Mayra said.

When I asked Mayra what she meant, Carmen answered, "They call us names and make fun of us because we are Latinas. Then we call them JAPs [Jewish-American princesses], and they get mad at us. This goes on in the corridors and also in the cafeteria."

I knew this conflict could escalate further and needed to cease now. How could I prevent the name-calling in the halls and cafeteria from happening in the future? How could I find a way to get the three students integrated into my classroom?

Questions

1. Explain this situation from the viewpoint of Carmen, Mayra, and Lucy. How do their views differ from Ann's? Is this issue a reflection of a schoolwide problem? If so, what are possible solutions?

2. What are the pros and cons of student choice in grouping? Make a list of both.
3. Think back to your own educational past. What kind of setting has most helped you learn: grouping by choice, teacher-assigned groups, or individual work? Why?
4. What other alternatives might Ann follow to foster respect for other cultures among the students? Explain.
5. How do you balance the needs of students to choose whom they work and socialize with and the needs of rejected students? Would your answer change based on the age of the students? For example, should kindergartners be able to say they don't want to play with certain children?

CASE 33

Flashback Pain

Pamela *Butler's cooperating teacher suggests that she explain to her sixth-grade class that she has a cleft palate. This brings back the pain Pamela felt years before at being denied the opportunity to teach.*

I had for decades this secret dream to be a certified teacher, so I was excited when I received my placement at a huge, urban middle school that accommodates more than 2,000 students. Although Mr. Kirby, my cooperating teacher, is male, younger than I (when you're 50, most people are younger), autocratic, and Marine-like in his manner, I was determined for the next four months to accept his guidance, criticism, and comments in a gracious manner. However, despite my efforts, I was to experience a situation that left me very upset.

I was born with a cleft palate and lip. I was a happy child, driven by a desire to be a teacher. In high school, all of my teachers knew of my condition and still encouraged me to be a math teacher. During this time, I tutored grammar school students in math, while I studied math in a college prep curricula. All looked well until I was accepted to a university and was informed that I could never be certified to teach because of the cleft palate. This was before the Americans with Disabilities Act was passed. So I switched gears and attended nursing school, but my desire to teach never evaporated.

As a nurse and administrator, I had many occasions to teach in the years that followed. When I became a substitute school nurse, I decided to take the opportunity the law now allowed for me to get my certification. I was interviewed by Mr. Kirby, his supervisor, and the principal prior to my acceptance at my assigned school. My cleft palate was mentioned during the interview, and Mr. Kirby's supervisor expressed concern about the discrimination of the '60s and '70s.

For my first two days in the classroom, all seemingly was going well. I ran errands, passed out books and supplies, and circulated through the class, answering questions or providing assistance. When I wasn't doing all this, I closely watched Mr. Kirby as he taught. I also studied the learners. They were a great bunch, and I looked forward to actually beginning teaching.

At the end of an exhausting second day at the school, Mr. Kirby informed me that due to my extensive background in health, it would be best to start teaching as soon as possible. I readily agreed. Then he told me that on my first day of teaching I would have to explain to the students that I have a cleft palate. I told him that I did not agree and thought it would be wiser to wait until the situation came up in a more natural way. He became obviously uptight and argued that students would go home and complain to their parents that they have a teacher who can't even talk right.

I only wish he had uttered those words during the interview. I then had the option of not accepting that assignment. In a controlled manner I told him I would give the matter some thought that evening and get back to him.

I am now at home, trying to decide what to do. I have spent the whole evening so far in flashback pain with memories of my days as a student and my great desire to teach. I truly don't know what course to take: accept what Mr. Kirby says to do, or go against him and follow my heart? Oh, the frustration and pain of not being understood!

Questions

1. Explain this dilemma from Mr. Kirby's point of view.
2. What resources, legal and otherwise, are available to Pamela in this case? What are the provisions of the Americans with Disabilities Act?
3. Does Pamela have to either accept what Mr. Kirby says or follow her heart? Can you think of other courses she might take?
4. What steps would you take as a teacher to ensure that a child with a disability in your class feels comfortable?
5. How does our background of experiences in school affect our teaching? Can you think of incidents that occurred during your schooling that have had an impact on your teaching now?

CASE 34

Am I Discriminating Against Amy?

Cindy Cox doesn't know what to do about Amy, a student who she feels is pushing her own religious ideas on the other students in her high school history class. She stops Amy from doing a paper on a religious topic, but when another student presents a paper on the Dalai Lama, Amy accuses her of discrimination.

Let me introduce myself to you. My name is Cindy Cox, and I pride myself on speaking my mind. Currently, I'm a student teacher at George Washington High School, a modern, limestone building in the beautiful Texas Hill Country, and if I may say so myself, I'm doing a pretty good job. My cooperating teacher is Ms. Cantu, who has been very supportive of my efforts to stimulate our history students to think critically. We make a great team.

This is my problem: In my teacher education classes, I was told to keep religion out of the classroom, and I totally agreed. After all, we have to separate church and state. So when my students first asked me what church I went to, I told them right then and there that my personal spiritual beliefs have nothing to do with what I am teaching them about American history. And the students seemed to accept that.

All of them, that is, except Amy.

Amy is a whole 'nother story! Until she got to high school, she was homeschooled by her parents, who belong to a fundamentalist religious group that has a lot of members around here. To be fair, she must have gotten a good education at home, because she seems to have a lot of confidence, writes well, and speaks in class often. But that's part of the problem! Amy speaks all the time! I don't mind her having her own beliefs, but she keeps putting down other students for not having her views. She calls people in some of the countries we study "heathens," says rock music is the work of the devil, and has argued against evolution. I do not know how to deal with this pill. When I asked Ms. Cantu, she said to just ignore her, but frankly I can't.

I had a great assignment for the class for their midterm paper, and I thought it might be a way to get Amy to stop and consider the viewpoints of others instead of pushing her own ideas down her classmates' throats. No such luck! The assignment was to write a paper on a person who has made a difference in the world. I believe in giving choice, so I didn't assign particular people. I thought there was no way that this kid could sneak her conservative religious ideas into a paper like this. Even if she chose someone like Mother Teresa, I thought, at least she'd learn something about an international figure who has indeed made a difference.

Major mistake. Amy decided she wanted to write about a nationally known evangelist associated with her own denomination. "He's made more difference than anyone else," Amy stubbornly asserted. I knew that this topic would just give her a platform to sound off her religious views once again, so I scheduled a conference with Amy. I suggested to her that she choose another subject, one that she was not so close to. That way she might learn something and, I couldn't resist adding, make a better grade. Amy reluctantly agreed and ended up writing on Betty Ford.

On the day that the class presented their papers to the class, I held my breath. I was being observed that day and worried that Amy might find a way to push her religious ideas somehow. My student teaching supervisor, Ms. Carleton, is a very nice woman, but I didn't want to chance it. I was worried how she'd react to Amy—and even more worried how she'd react to my reacting to Amy.

Luckily, Amy's paper turned out to be just fine. She had actually done a good job of researching Betty Ford and her contributions. I held my breath until the paper was over, but Amy came out with flying colors. She answered her classmates' questions with confidence. It was obvious that she knew her topic. As she sat down, I relaxed for the first time in days.

But just when I thought things were going well, everything exploded in my face. Janice was giving her report on the Dalai Lama, explaining that he had won the Nobel Prize and had devoted himself to trying to bring about world peace. I was impressed with all the books she had read on Tibet and on the Dalai Lama, and I noticed that Ms. Carleton was nodding her approval. Just then, though, Amy got me back for not letting her write about her evangelist. It was during the question and answer period. Standing up with her hands planted on her hips and looking straight at me, she said, "Miss Cox, you're discriminating. Why could Janice give her report on a religious topic, but I couldn't?"

I was so taken aback that I didn't answer right away, but that didn't bother Amy. She just asked again, "Why am I told that when I say something about Christianity that it's somehow not OK, but Janice is encouraged to spread non-Christianity?" As all eyes, including those of Ms. Carleton, turned on me, I began to think frantically. What could I answer? What was Ms. Carleton thinking about me? Was I discriminating against Amy?

Questions

1. Does separation of church and state mean that students should not be allowed to express their religious views? Explain.
2. What difference, if any, is there between expressing religious views and proselytizing?
3. Should there be limits to student freedom of choice? If so, what should these limits be?
4. Do you think the student teacher would have handled Amy's question differently if her supervisor had not been present? What role, in your opinion, should a supervisor play?

For Further Reading

American Association of University Women. (1995). *How schools shortchange girls.* New York: Marlowe.

> This pamphlet examines research showing that males receive more teacher attention than females do. This is the case, the authors suggest, for children in elementary grades through college.

Bigelow, B., Christensen, L., Karp, S., Miner, B., & Petersen, B. (Eds.). (1994). *Rethinking our classrooms: Teaching for equity and justice* [Special edition of *Rethinking Schools*]. Milwaukee: Rethinking Schools.

> This collection of resources, handouts, lesson plans, poems, and teaching tips is practical in nature but very compelling in philosophy. It is a thoughtful statement of how we can help children in crisis at the classroom level.

Erikson, E. (1968). *Identity, youth, and crisis.* New York: Norton.

> This is a pioneering work on the concept of identity and identity crisis. The author challenges the Freudian view that the ego is fixed in early childhood and instead posits a series of developmental phases—from infancy and continuing throughout a lifetime—through which the subject resolves conflicts such as that over establishing trust or achieving autonomy.

Fine, M. (1995). *Habits of mind: Struggling over values in America's classroom.* San Francisco: Jossey-Bass.

> This book offers valuable insights into ways in which teachers and students might begin to understand and deal with multiracial differences.

Gearheart, B. R., Weishahn, M. W., & Gearheart, C. J. (1996). *The exceptional student in the regular classroom* (6th ed.). Upper Saddle River, NJ: Merrill/Prentice Hall.

> This college textbook provides a solid overview of inclusion, emphasizing the needs of special learners and how regular classroom teachers can effectively meet those needs. The book includes a brief history of education for people with disabilities, pertinent legislation, characteristics of exceptionalities, and effective instructional strategies.

Gilyard, K. (1991). *Voices of the self.* Detroit: Wayne State University Press.

> This book functions as both theoretical treatise and personal memoir as the author discusses and analyzes his own struggle to develop language competence by code switching between black English and standard English. The work offers important lessons for those involved in the education of African-American students.

Harbeck, K. (Ed.). (1992). *Coming out of the classroom closet: Gay and lesbian students, teachers and curricula.* New York: Harrington Park.

> This collection of essays looks at the damaging effects of homophobia and silence about lesbian and gay identity in schools.

hooks, b. (1989). *Talking back: Thinking feminist, thinking black.* Boston: South End.

> These essays are autobiographical reflections focusing on African-American female identity. Hooks describes the process of coming to voice as a revolutionary gesture, a way for African-Americans and other oppressed peoples to problematize dominant assumptions, to resist, to talk back.

Maslow, A. (1970). *Motivation and personality* (2nd ed.). New York: Harper & Row. [Originally published in 1954]

In this classic work by the founder of the humanistic movement in education, Maslow describes two groups of human needs arranged in a hierarchy that shows the interrelationship of social, physical, emotional, and intellectual and aesthetic needs.

Morely, D., & Chen, K. H. (Eds.). (1996). *Stuart Hall: Critical dialogues in cultural studies.* New York: Routledge.

This collection provides an in-depth look at the concept of identity politics as developed by theorist Stuart Hall. Essays include Hall's "Gramsci's Relevance for the Study of Race and Ethnicity," "New Ethnicities," and "What Is This 'Black' in Black Popular Culture?"

Ruenzel, D. (1994, September 11). Coming out. *Education Week*, pp. 22–26.

This article tells the story of a Missouri teacher, Rodney Wilson, who came out as a gay man to his students and was harassed by the administration of his school even though the majority of his students supported him and none of the parents complained.

SECTION 4

Challenges of Working with Families

CASE 35

Rebecca's Ways

Dolores *Gonzales feels that Rebecca, a three-year-old child in her preschool class, has medical problems that need to be addressed. She wonders what the best ways are to approach the child's mother for more information and what can be done to help Rebecca in the classroom.*

I have been closely observing Rebecca since the beginning of the semester, and I think she's getting worse. Rebecca is a three-year-old girl who has poor vision, tantrums, and perhaps a bit of a hearing loss. Whenever Rebecca doesn't get her way, or whenever we have transitions from circle time to outside time, she screams, kicks, flails her arms, and often throws herself on the floor. When I try to pick her up, she tenses her body so that it is difficult to hold her. My cooperating teacher, Vicki, has been trying to reason with her, but if she doesn't calm down enough so that we can talk to her, we have to put her in the library corner on the soft rug, among the pillows, until she gains control of herself.

When Vicki mentioned the difficulty we are having with Rebecca's tantrums, her mother replied, "Oh, she gets that from her cousin," but could not offer us advice on how she helps Rebecca calm down at home.

After this talk with her mother, Vicki said to me, "I don't think she could be learning this from a cousin since she is doing this every day. She is just not with her cousin that often." I also felt that Rebecca was truly out of control, not just putting on an act. Vicki and I both feel that her physical problems are contributing to her low tolerance for frustration and her difficulty with classroom activities and routines.

For example, Rebecca has a lazy eye and possibly other vision problems. She wears glasses for correction and sunglasses outside, but she seems to always squint; and when trying to reach for items, she usually misses them. Although she can differentiate shapes and letters well, she seems mystified by color differences. This leads us to wonder if she is having difficulty actually seeing the colors properly.

When we asked Rebecca's mother about this, she said, "Maybe she needs a new prescription. These glasses may be too old, but I can't take her to the doctor right now." Later the mother mentioned that she had gotten new glasses for Rebecca, but the child continues to wear the same old pair to school.

We are also concerned about Rebecca's hearing. Whenever we ask her a question or tell her something, she replies, "Huh?" Her mother believes that Rebecca just has selective hearing and doesn't pay attention because she doesn't want to.

Vicki is planning a conference with Rebecca's mother to get permission to speak with Rebecca's doctor and have the child tested further. She feels we are not being told everything and that our information may help the doctor in treating Rebecca. We are crossing our fingers that Rebecca's mother will agree. I never anticipated this kind of situation before I started student teaching. It really has opened my eyes and left me wondering if I have the observation skill, patience, and understanding to work with a child who may have problems, and especially with parents. What is the best approach to take with Rebecca's mom?

Questions

1. What is Rebecca's mother's viewpoint? How might she tell her version of this case?
2. What possible ways can the teachers help Rebecca with her tantrums? How many alternatives can you think of? What role can the student teacher play?
3. What other information about Rebecca, including medical information, would you like to know if you were the teacher? Why?
4. What things need to be considered when working with a parent whose child is having difficulties?
5. What other professionals in your school or your municipality could you turn to for help with Rebecca?

CASE 36

Don't Give Up on Elvin

Cassie Corbin, a student teacher in an inner-city kindergarten class, feels that her cooperating teacher has given up on Elvin, who has many problems in school. She gets no support from his father either, but she desperately wants to save Elvin from becoming just one more inner-city child who doesn't make it.

The classroom I'm working in for my student teaching is in the basement of the South First Street School. The majority of the surrounding urban community is African-American with an economic status at the poverty level. Crime and teenage pregnancy rates are very high, and there is a persistent drug problem.

I chose this school because I want to make a difference in the lives of the children in this community. I am grateful for my own education and want to help other African-Americans succeed. Some of the children in my kindergarten class have severe problems. One child eats out of the garbage. Another cries for his mother four days out of the week. Three of the students, Charles, Tome, and Delores, live with their grandmothers and call them mother. They have no contact with either of their parents. Most of the students, however, seem emotionally secure about attending school.

My student teaching experience is going well except that I can't get Elvin off my mind. Elvin would be labeled "at risk." In my opinion, his father contributes to the problem. He will not bring Elvin to school on a regular basis, saying only that he "didn't feel like it" or that "the bus never came." Whenever I talk to him about Elvin's behavior, he just shrugs his shoulders, and nothing is ever done.

My cooperating teacher, Ms. Cohen, lets Elvin get away with everything, commenting to me, "I give up; I'm tired of trying to discipline him." At first, being the new asset to the class, I thought I could solve everything. After all, I had enthusiasm and caring on my side, and I was determined to make a difference. Yet no matter what I tried, Elvin continued to misbehave. Why should he listen to a student teacher if his regular teacher lets him do whatever he wants?

I think Ms. Cohen has given up on him too quickly. I think that Elvin needs to know that it's a tough world that awaits him out there and that no one else is going to be so easy on him. Still, Ms. Cohen's been here for over 20 years, and maybe she has seen it all. Besides, I am afraid to confront her because I don't think that is the place of a student teacher.

Meanwhile, Elvin defies every name in the book, and I have trouble not thinking of him as a problem child. He gives new meaning to the name "Dennis the Menace." He will sit next to anyone and start trouble. He talks back to the teacher. He ties his shoelaces together and can't get them apart. He puts his food in his hair. He stands on his chair and runs away when I ask him to sit down. He is very untidy. If I threaten to put him in the hall or take him to another classroom, he says, "Okay, please let me go!" During naptime, he jumps up and down, throwing his sheets and shouting, "I want to get up." When I try to punish Elvin, he thinks it is funny. He even asks to be punished!

I still care about Elvin and worry about what awaits him in later life. I refuse to give up on him or communicate to him that I have low expectations. Someone has to do something or else Elvin will become another statistic in this community. So I'm left wondering, what should I do now? My cooperating teacher has given up hope. Elvin's father doesn't want to listen to me because I'm only the student teacher. I'm beginning to wonder if I'm being too idealistic and whether I really can make a difference.

Questions

1. Do you believe that teachers can make a difference with children who are at risk? Explain. Do you think that the term *at risk* is appropriate? Are there some children who are indeed at risk?
2. What are some of the strategies that Cassie has tried with Elvin? Why do you think they have not been successful?
3. What do you think are the reasons explaining why Elvin behaves the way he does? Write a paragraph describing school from his perspective and from his father's perspective. Does this give you any new insights?
4. What role does your knowledge of child development play in deciding what you would do in this situation? How does Elvin's being a kindergartner affect your decisions?
5. What effect do teacher expectations have on Elvin in this case? How can student teachers become aware of the effect that their own expectations have on their students?

CASE 37

Homework Hassles

> ***Mr.*** *Bachman is surprised during fourth-grade parent-teacher conferences that so many parents describe homework as a problem and a nightly battle. He wonders whether homework is worth the negative energy and how homework can be more positive and productive.*

As I look back over my first experience in observing and participating in fourth-grade parent-teacher conferences, which were held last week, I am frustrated by the over-riding theme: *homework.* I heard over and over again, "Mr. Bachman, I just don't know what to do. It is such a struggle to get my child to do homework. It becomes a nightly battle." I have also received several notes lately from parents asking me to reteach material to their children because they didn't understand it when it was presented in class. This mostly occurs in math, and I think parents and children are often frustrated because the parents are unable to help.

I am student teaching in a middle-sized suburban school in a predominantly white, working-class town. I am making a career change; having already raised my own children, I can see the culture of schools through both my grandchildren's experience and through my teacher preparation program. From this perspective, I think one thing that causes frustration in parents is the way in which math instruction has changed since they were in grade school. Even my peers in our teacher education program have expressed frustration about trying to teach math because methods have changed so much, and it really takes a great deal of preparation to be successful.

The homework problem is showing up with all types of students, including the "good" ones who do hand in homework on a consistent basis. When a parent, during conferences, described horrific scenes that take place at homework time, my cooperating teachers and I were many times very surprised because the child being described was often an industrious worker in class. So in my eyes the problem comes down to this: there seems to be an awful lot of negative energy expended by students, parents, and teachers on the issue of homework in terms of its completion and collection. What can I do to channel this energy into a positive form?

My first choice might be to leave it alone and just continue with the homework battles. Homework has been around as long as dirt, and some people feel that our children are just lazy and won't want to do anything unless it's easy or feels good. Many feel that homework is necessary because it gives the students time to practice concepts and skills that they have learned during the school day. After all, there are homework hot lines and teachers willing to help students after school with lessons. There are also basic skills departments in school to help students who are having difficulty in the core subjects. Just accepting homework the way it is comes from the "if it isn't broken, don't fix it" school of thought.

Of course, given my experiences so far in this school, I think something really is broken. Perhaps homework should just be abolished. An analogy can be made that when adults finish their work for the day, they are able to come home and relax. Children should be able to do the same. If they have put in a hard day's work on their studies, they should be able to use their evening for relaxation; self-enriching activities such as sports, music, dance, scouts, or religious education; or just spending time with their families in a nonadversarial environment rather than the stressful one created by homework battles.

Perhaps parents and students are overbooked and are trying to do too much, with the result that everyone feels mad and guilty when these schedules wear everyone thin. Parents are exhausted from working and from taking their children to all of the different activities that they are involved in. The children are not allowed to be just kids anymore, having their days filled with structured activities from 7 A.M. to 8 P.M. No wonder they don't feel like doing homework. I teach piano lessons at night, and it is very difficult to arrange lesson times because of the students' breakneck schedules. I wonder if children are really benefiting from these activities and whether they are able to focus on homework. Or is everyone just caught up in this endurance race?

As a student teacher, I have been wrestling with these ideas and continue with my sense of uneasiness about how homework is handled. What can I do to make it more productive? And always in the back of my mind I wonder, "What will I do in my own classroom?"

Questions

1. In your experiences so far in teaching, do you think homework plays a positive role? Why? Why not?
2. Have you found that there are students who consistently don't hand in homework? How do you handle this? Is your method successful at getting students to start doing homework?
3. What do you know about the lives of the children in your class after school? How does this affect their ability to do homework? What other factors affect whether the students are successful in doing the homework?
4. What other issues are important in this case? Do you think math is more of a homework problem than other subjects are?
5. What advice would you give Mr. Bachman? What do you plan to do about homework? What institutional constraints do you have?

CASE 38

Using Ritalin: Whose Decision Is It?

Mark *Campos attends a meeting about Kenny, one of his 6th-grade students, in which the teachers try to convince Kenny's mother to consider Ritalin to help control his behavior.*

I wasn't sure what to expect when I was asked to attend a meeting about Kenny. In this middle school where I was student teaching, we worked in teams, called T-sets, for thematic planning and to provide a stable set of teachers for each cohort of students. In other words, there were four teachers from different content areas that taught the same group of students. Therefore, all of the teachers in our team were at the meeting, as well as the school psychologist, the assistant principal and Kenny's mother. I was there with my cooperating teacher just for the experience of it. I had decided long ago that keeping my mouth shut was often the best course in student teaching.

The meeting centered on how to help Kenny's sometimes uncontrollable behavior. The other teachers felt strongly that he should be given Ritalin, a drug that helped hyperactive and inattentive children to concentrate better. Kenny had already been left back once, early in his elementary years. I don't think he had a special education classification, because I assume I would have known that. His work this year in 6th grade was inconsistent. He had some good grades, and poor ones, but it was his behavior that brought us all to this meeting. The other teachers made a case that Ritalin was the only way Kenny could be controlled in class, and the only hope for his academic performance to improve.

My own observations of Kenny somewhat supported this. If I gave him attention, he would stay with me. He seemed rather bright to me in fact. As long as I was physically present or directly engaging Kenny, he caught on to concepts and did his work well. It would have been fine if there weren't 25 other students in the room! The minute I walked away from Kenny, I would lose him. At best he would wiggle out of his seat, wander around the room, stare out the window, play with his other books and papers. At worst, he would talk to other students, take their things, and even sing and crack jokes. I never felt it was a physical or perceptual problem, though. It seemed more emotional to me, and I often wondered if it was from a lack of attention from his mother.

Kenny lived with his mother and younger brother. There was never any mention of a father, and the best way I can describe his mother is disconnected from her children. She seemed to be the type of parent that wouldn't normally be involved in her kid's schooling, but this issue forced her to be. She sat unhappily in the midst of this intimidating group of professionals. She wasn't very knowledgeable about "school things," and I suppose from her fear or frustration she wasn't very cooperative, either.

In this school many students were already taking Ritalin as well as other medications. This never seemed right to me; I worried it was being abused. But as I sat and listened to the other teachers, and thought about Kenny's behavior in my class, I was hoping they could convince his mother to at least try the Ritalin. For the first time, I was seeing the other side of this problem, and it seemed like this drug was really the answer.

Kenny's mother was defensive. She must have felt that she was being blamed in some way, and this made her reluctant to listen to us. I didn't understand, really, why she wouldn't want to try this. She admitted that Kenny's behavior at home was occasionally a problem, but somehow she didn't want to acknowledge that any of it was serious enough to take this next step.

As I sat listening to the discussion, I wondered about whose decision this should be. Did the teachers have the right to push so hard for using medication? Shouldn't this be a decision between Kenny's mother and his doctor? On the other hand, I was hoping Kenny's mother would at least talk to Kenny's doctor about this problem. Somehow, the whole meeting was unsettling to me—and I wondered how I would handle such a situation when I was on my own.

Questions

1. Do you have children in your class or school who are taking Ritalin? What have been the results? What are some side effects of this drug to look for?
2. What else could the teachers do to help Kenny without using drugs?
3. Do you think that teachers should recommend Ritalin to parents? Why? Why not?
4. How could the relationship between Kenny's mother and the school be improved? What could have been done to establish a more positive relationship before this meeting?
5. Why do you think so many children are using Ritalin in our schools?

CASE 39

Not My Kid

Carmela doesn't know what to do when a mother challenges the way that she is teaching and questions the revisions her daughter has been asked to make to an assignment.

I was really enjoying my student teaching when I ran into a snag with Julia's mother. I loved this school—a modern, progressive school just outside the city boundaries. The families came from mixed socioeconomic levels, and about half of the kids were white—creating a nice balance of diversity in my mind. The parents were pretty involved in the school. The PTA was active, and we had good attendance at back-to-school night. Whenever we asked for volunteers, we got plenty of help. I was quite impressed by the parents because my previous experience had been in an urban school where lack of parental involvement was a real problem.

The classes were ability grouped, and I was teaching social studies to two middle-level 7th grades and one high-level 8th-grade class. Julia was in my 8th-grade class, and she was clearly a high achiever. I enjoyed these students because they were always willing to be challenged. It was rewarding to see them learn so much. I sometimes got the feeling they could learn as well without me—I was only there to organize the activities to keep them on track.

We were in the middle of a long unit on early American history. I wanted the students to research the life and work of one of the early U.S. presidents. I was also trying to minimize use of the textbook and have the students make good use of the Internet instead. We had done a few lessons already on searching for information, evaluating the information, and how it could be used in their reports. I had previewed many sites and had provided data sheets with these sites as a place for the students to start.

The problem began when Julia handed in her report. I had seen this information before—recognized the photos and text—and realized she had just printed out some pages from the Internet. The report was just unauthentic—even for a bright 8th grader like Julia. I easily found the site she had used and confirmed that it was copied directly.

After conferring with my cooperating teacher, I talked to Julia about it, explaining that we wanted her to do more than just copy and print information from the Internet. I went over the strengths in some of her report, but told her the copied pages were unacceptable and needed to be redone. I would not grade her paper until it was revised. I thought I was being generous and lenient.

A few days later, I was in my dorm room when the phone rang. To my surprise, it was Julia's mother. She was very upset with criticism of Julia's work and rambled on about how smart Julia is. During this long, detailed discussion, she told me what stipulations and guidelines I should have used. I interpreted her message as saying that I was just a student teacher and had overstepped my boundaries. To be honest, I could hardly defend or explain myself, I was so shocked. My confidence was shaken, and I couldn't help but think that teachers who wanted parent input didn't know what they were asking for!

What was I to do now?

Questions

1. What do you think Carmela should do? How should she respond to Julia's mother?
2. Do you agree with the way Carmela handled the copying that Julia did? What else could she have done?
3. What suggestions do you have for preventing the problem of copying from the Internet? What guidelines should be used? How would these guidelines change based on the age of the students?
4. What do you think is the appropriate amount of parent involvement? How much and in what ways should parents be involved?
5. How can student teachers best handle the issue of being perceived as "not the real teacher"?

CASE **40**

The Movie Controversy: Beyond the Rating

Rita *Uribe runs into a controversy while teaching her 10th-grade U.S. history class. The parents will not give their permission for the class to go see the movie Beloved, and Rita questions their reasons and what to do about the situation.*

I never imagined that planning good lessons could be so controversial! My goal for my two 10th-grade U.S. history classes was to have them take other people's perspectives and understand other races and cultures. Our school is somewhat diverse— one of my classes, for example, has four African-American students, four Latinos, two Asians, and 14 whites. I, however, am the only African-American teacher in the school. Our textbook is a good one, as far as textbooks go, but I was determined to use other ways of getting my students excited about history and more important, to be able to relate history to their own lives.

When we began studying about slavery in the United States, I thought that taking them to see the film *Beloved* would be ideal for our curriculum. The movie portrays a story about slavery that is highly symbolic and would generate a lot of discussion. It would give them a common experience that we could use as a springboard for looking at broader issues. I was worried that it might be "above their heads," but I realize now that the controversy was focused on the scenes in which slaves get raped and whipped and full body parts are shown. The realism, though, was an important part of the effect that I felt was necessary to get the students both intellectually and emotionally involved in history.

My cooperating teacher, Mr. Carnahan, was very supportive of the idea, even though we both admitted this would be a controversial issue. Obviously the parents needed to give their consent, so we drafted a letter together that clearly explained our academic reasons for seeing the film and how it would be incorporated into our curriculum. We also left room for parents' comments on the permission slips that were to be returned to us.

I guess the parents' reactions shouldn't have surprised me, but I wanted so badly for them to approve, that I was more than a little upset. Just over half of the parents objected to the field trip, saying that the movie was inappropriate for high school students. A few parents actually mentioned the nudity as the problem.

I think this was a cover-up though. These parents didn't want their children to deal with slavery in a blunt, raw way. There were no happy slave images that I had often been exposed to in my own education. My feeling was that the parents, perhaps subconsciously, wanted to keep it hushed up, especially as it related to sexuality. What made me so angry, though, was the idea that parents wouldn't want to expose their kids to cultural history and heritage in a guided, structured environment that the school could provide, but they allowed their children to see other movies that were, in my mind, violent and disgusting. If these were kids who only went to PG-13 movies, then I might have reacted differently!

So now that I have gotten back these permission slips, it is quite apparent that we don't have enough support for the field trip. I'm wondering, though, what do I do now? Do I just forget about the whole thing? Should I discuss the parents' reactions with the students? And what could I do in the future to convince parents about the value of this film?

Questions

1. Do you think the movie *Beloved* is appropriate to include as part of a 10th-grade U.S. history curriculum? Why? Why not? What basis do you use to make this decision?
2. How would you interpret the parents' reactions in this case? Do you agree with Rita's interpretation?
3. How much input should parents have in any curriculum? In what ways are parents involved in decision making in your school?
4. In what ways do students' developmental levels affect their understanding of history and social studies in general?
5. What other curriculum suggestions can you give Rita? What should she do now?

CASE **41**

Pressure to Succeed

Janice worries about the pressure that parents put on her high school students. Not only are they under pressure to perform well academically but they are busy with many activities outside of school. She wonders if she should speak to the parents about her concerns.

I always wanted to be a teacher, ever since I was a child, but my family couldn't afford the cost of giving me a higher education. So after 10 years of working in the business sector, I decided to go to college to fulfill my lifetime dream. My college experience was wonderful. I was serious about my studies and worked hard to do well, and my professors knew it. I did better than I had ever imagined I would.

Then I started my internship. I taught a biology class of 10th and 11th graders in Richland Heights, a rich part of town. The school was a nice one, and Miss Burns, my cooperating teacher, acted more like a friend than anything else. She was always there for me and gave me many handy tips for planning lessons, which I appreciated greatly. Actually, everyone went out of their way to welcome me to the school. During Black History Month, I was honored to be invited to speak before the whole faculty about the contributions of my culture to present-day music and literature, and the principal, Mr. Parkman, publicly praised me for my talk.

My class was made up of typical teenagers. I had a lot of hands-on work. Some of them got it; others had a much harder time. I prided myself in being fair, though. I worked just as hard with the underachievers as those who did well. I wanted to teach everyone, regardless of their level or abilities, and let them know I cared that they learned. I believe that the students appreciated my fairness and responded to the attention I gave them. I was used to hard work, always came prepared, and maintained an orderly classroom. In general, this was a very smooth experience.

What bothered me didn't really have anything to do with my teaching. It had to do with the parents. These parents were something else. When I was a kid, my time was my own. I just played with my sisters and brothers or, when I was a teenager, hung out with my friends. I didn't have any planned activities after school, and if I didn't do my homework, it was my problem. Sure I'd get in big trouble if my grades were bad, but it was my responsibility to keep up, study for my tests, and do well in school. My parents worked too hard and had too many kids to be constantly worrying about our grades or especially about our social situation. And I am grateful for that. I think it toughened us up and helped us live in the real world.

Things must have changed since I was in school, though. Here the parents were always in the school, talking to the principal, talking to the teacher, talking to the counselor. They would argue about the grades their kids brought home and accuse you if they were low. Not that they wanted the teachers to be easy, though. The teachers they liked the best were the ones that were the hardest. They just wanted their kids to do better than anybody else in the hardest classes.

What bugged me, though, was not the pressure on me and the other teachers. I could deal with that. I have high expectations of my classes and am definitely not an easy touch. What I didn't like was the pressure on the students themselves. If the teachers were under pressure to make sure the students made good grades, the students were doubly under pressure from their parents. Students told me they were grounded for even making Bs! You wouldn't believe it! More than once, I saw young people mortified when their parents came to the school to complain about their grades—or even the results of the cheerleading tryouts or class beauties.

Despite my efforts to make biology fun and interesting, my students were always yawning in class. When I asked them why they were so tired all the time, they told me they had to go to piano lessons or football practice or private tutoring when school was out, then do their homework afterward—regardless of what time it was. Sometimes they'd have more than one of these activities in one night. You'd have thought six hours of learning a day would be enough. I couldn't understand why their days had to be so long. Why couldn't they have a childhood?

Anyway, I wondered whether any of this was my business. Should I have raised my reservations about all this pressure on these students at the parent-teacher conferences? It wasn't anything that was happening in my classroom, but it certainly had an effect. Didn't I have a responsibility to my class? When I asked Miss Burns what she thought, she shrugged and told me she thought the whole thing was crazy, too.

Questions

1. What would you do in this student teacher's situation?
2. Try to envision this situation from the standpoint of the parents. Does this change your own view any? Explain.
3. What might the student teacher do to help the students themselves?
4. What do you believe is the ideal level of parent involvement in school?

CASE 42

Discipline on Your Time, Not Mine

Jackie Harris gives detention to Kareem, one of her high school students whose behavior she finds unacceptable. Kareem's mother is upset with the punishment and refuses to help with his behavior.

Kareem's mother didn't want to see me; she would only talk to the "real" teacher. I tried not to let this bother me as much as it did, but I was frustrated. For weeks now I had been completely in charge of my 9th- and 10th-grade English classes. Kareem was therefore my responsibility on a practical level, and I was being treated like I didn't matter.

Kareem is the class clown. He is a very sweet kid, but he makes sure the attention always revolves around him. He is also very sensitive. For example, if he was reading aloud and couldn't pronounce a word, I could never correct him—he would be embarrassed all out of proportion to the importance of the activity. Perhaps because of his lack of self-esteem in academics, he often did not participate in class, nor pay attention. He would respond with, "I don't want to answer that. . . ." Or simply say no in defiance of any request. Occasionally he would get nasty, acting rude and cursing at me and others. A few days ago, I decided this cursing at me had to stop. I had to let Kareem know when his behavior was unacceptable, so I gave him afterschool detention.

This is what got Kareem's mother so angry. He didn't stay for detention that day as he was supposed to because he needed to pick up his younger brother in elementary school and bring him home after school. Although I had tried to contact her previously about Kareem's behavior with both notes and phone calls, none of these was answered. This time, however, she initiated the contact and asked for a meeting. My cooperating teacher, Ms. Stewart, the assistant principal, Mr. Johnson, and I joined her. She came in with her own agenda—and angry and disgruntled. She defended her son and complained that the detention he was given was unfair and inappropriate.

I tried to explain why the punishment was needed, but she made it clear that she wanted to speak to my cooperating teacher. Thankfully, Ms. Stewart supported me and kept trying to explain to her that Kareem could not get away scot-free when he was out of line. He needed to be disciplined, and the school's policy was afterschool detention. As Kareem's mother got more agitated and rude, Mr. Johnson, a large and intimidating man who also coached and played football, took over the situation.

Finally, Kareem's mother blurted out, "You do whatever you have to with Kareem, but not on my time!" We would have to find another way to discipline him because the afterschool time could not be cut into. And morning was out too. She needed him at home then.

Mr. Johnson finally closed the meeting by suggesting other possibilities, like giving up lunch. I was still frustrated though. It was like she was missing the whole point of the issue and didn't really care about Kareem's behavior at all as long as it didn't interfere with her life. I wondered how we would ever get through to Kareem when we obviously had no support from her.

I returned to the classroom, and Kareem's behavior, knowing that I was really on my own. How could I get Kareem's behavior to improve? Punishment was not going to work, now. What else could I do? And how could I get Kareem's mother to understand that we needed to be partners rather than adversaries?

Questions

1. What else can Jackie do about Kareem's behavior without using punishment? Do you think detention is effective? Why? Why not?
2. How can Jackie turn things around with Kareem's mother? How can they establish more of a partnership, as Jackie wants?
3. Retell this story as if you were Kareem's mother. What is her perspective? Are there other issues in this case that haven't been brought out in the narrative above?
4. Do you think the issues in this case are only relevant to high school? In what ways would you expect the teacher to act differently if the students were younger?
5. What else would you want to know about Kareem and this situation to make a better choice of what to do next?

For Further Reading

Armstrong, T. (1997). *The myth of the A.D.D child: 50 ways to improve your child's behavior and attention span without drugs, labels, or coercion*, Plume.

> This book challenges current diagnoses of attention deficit disorder and offers ways to deal with hyperactivity and short attention spans through practical strategies rather than drugs.

Berger, E. (1999). *Parents as partners in education: Families and schools working together.* Upper Saddle River, NJ: Prentice Hall.

> This textbook reviews past and current research, special concerns and challenges of working with minority and culturally diverse families, school- and home-based programs, the importance of good two-way communication, conducting parent conferences, involving parents of children with disabilities, dealing with child abuse and its aftermath, and such topics as advocacy and the rights-responsibilities balance. It is a comprehensive view of the field that puts theory into practical strategies.

Cooper, H. (1994). *The battle over homework: An administrator's guide to setting sound and effective policies.* Thousand Oaks, CA: Corwin.

> This book presents workable solutions to the dilemma over homework, drawing from research and interviews with principals, teachers, parents, and students. It is a comprehensive resource that looks at homework carefully and realistically.

Elkind, D. (1988). *The hurried child: Growing up too fast too soon.* Reading, MA: Addison-Wesley.

> Elkind warns us of the dangers of hurrying our children and gives us insight into the world of children in terms of education, television, social trends, and so on. The book is filled with advice on how we meet the needs of children and fight the crippling effects of pressure to achieve.

Kravolvec, E., & Buell, J. (2000). *The end of homework: How homework disrupts families, overburdens children and limits learning.* Beacon Press: Boston.

> These authors show the ways that homework can have negative consequences. They advocate for the importance of protecting children's leisure time and offer ways for schools to meet the goals of homework in more positive ways.

Lewis, R. B., & Doorlag, D. H. (1999). *Teaching special students in general education classrooms* (5th ed.). Upper Saddle River, NJ: Merrill/Prentice Hall.

> This very readable text was written from the practitioner's point of view and provides many instructional techniques for students with learning problems. Included are a thorough discussion of the Individuals with Disabilities Education Act and the Americans with Disabilities Act as well as information about attention deficit disorder (ADD) and attention deficit-hyperactivity disorder (ADHD).

Shockey, B., Michalove, N., & Allen, J. (1995). *Engaging families: Connecting home and school literacy communities.* Portsmouth, NH: Heinemann.

> These authors describe positive family partnerships and offer suggestions on creating an extended literacy community using the voices of children and parents.

Stafford, S., & Green, V. (1996). Preschool integration: Strategies for teachers. *Childhood Education, Infancy Through Early Adolescence, 72*(4), 214–218.

This article reviews integration, mainstreaming, inclusion, and least-restrictive environment and provides a program model for integration with many practical strategies.

Taylor, D., & Dorsey-Gaines, C. (1988). *Growing up literate: Learning from inner city families.* Portsmouth, NH: Heinemann.

This study of urban black children living in poverty focuses on how they were successfully learning to read and write despite their extraordinary economic hardships. The book present new images of the strengths of the family as educator and surprising conclusions.

SECTION 5

Challenges of Ethical Dilemmas

CASE 43

Do Not Touch

Marta *Cruzero, in her second month of student teaching in the third grade, has second thoughts about hugging a child who needs it or patting the children's shoulders when they are not paying attention. How can she use touch in an appropriate manner without being afraid of lawsuits concerning child molestation. How can she find a balance of when not to touch and when it's okay?*

Well, it's October, and I am getting to know Ms. Crichton's class of 18 students. I was placed in an award-winning school with an ethnically diverse population in a suburban area close to my home. I felt privileged to be in this school because of the awards it has won and because I wanted to work with students of different backgrounds.

All of my college teacher preparation courses gave me great confidence in the lessons that I wanted to teach, but I was not prepared for my doubts about when it was appropriate to touch a child.

This all started about the second or third week of student teaching, when Timothy came up to me to say good-bye at the end of the day. When he reached out and hugged me, I felt surprised by his affection. I didn't know how to react. I thought about the love this child felt and how he needed to express it. The next day, Timothy cheerfully said, "Good morning, Ms. Cruzero." He came up to hug me, and he really looked happy to see me. Teresa also came up to me to say, "Good morning," and she also hugged me. This gave me a feeling of appreciation, and I was happy to see the sensitivity in these children. That same day, as I was leaving to go to the multipurpose room, Timothy came up to me again to say good-bye and gave me a hug. I thought about him for a little while and wondered if he did not get much affection at home. I began to think that I was helping to fulfill a need that he had.

Then another situation occurred the next morning. Timothy came up to Ms. Crichton to hug her, and she seemed to look at him in an odd way and subtly pulled away from him. It was not very obvious, but I certainly noticed it. It seemed inappropriate to me because I was forming the opinion that Timothy really needed this affection.

One day I met Timothy outside the school, and he came up right away and hugged me. He was excited to see me, and I felt I was being idolized by this child. He introduced me to his sister, Tatiana. She looked at me like I was somebody special to Timothy.

I asked Timothy, "What are you doing playing here by the school?"

He proudly answered, "Oh, I live across the street from the school, over there."

"Does your mom know where you are?" I questioned.

"Oh, sure." he replied. I hoped it was true.

Another day, when I went shopping for my own son's clothes, I saw him across the store. Timothy spotted me right away, and he came over and introduced me to his mom. I talked to her for a few minutes and immediately felt that I had judged her unfairly; she struck me as a very caring mother. In fact, as they walked away from me in front of the store, she wrapped her arm around his shoulders and pulled him close.

After that day, my theory of Timothy's need for affection changed. I thought about it deeply and decided that it was just normal for a child to come to a teacher for a hug. I also thought about my own children and how a child needs to express his or her feelings. This made me aware of my own feelings, bringing back memories of my childhood when I did not receive much affection at home.

Now I am left with questions and discomfort about the appropriate amount, if any, of hugging and touching that teachers should use. On the one hand, I understand the concern about inappropriate touching. I am a parent myself and worry about how my own children are treated. On the other hand, I think children need affection and that touch is very important. Now I wonder if it is all right to use my hands to get a child's attention, like patting him on the shoulder? How about using my hands to control a child who is about to hurt someone? Are hugs appropriate? Don't all children need hugs? Where do we draw the line, both legally and ethically?

Questions

1. What is the policy about touching children at your school? Has this been presented to you formally? Is there an informal standard? How do you decide what is appropriate in the classroom you are student teaching in?
2. Do you think that teachers should be able to hug children? Should both male and female teachers hug children? Why? Why not?
3. What effect does the age of the child have on your feelings about appropriate touches? Would it be all right to hug a five-year-old who is upset? Help a two-year-old pull down her pants? Comfort a 10-year-old who has been frightened? Hug a teenager who has won a scholarship to college?
4. In what way does Erikson's theory of psychosocial development help us understand the child's need for touch? Does this theory add insight to your answer to question 3? How does Maslow's hierarchy of needs help us to understand this issue?
5. What ideas have you formed about the parents of the children in your class? Do you think you are making a fair assessment? On what are you basing your judgments? How much do you know about the families of the children in your class? How has this information helped you or changed your interactions with the children?

CASE 44

Stop Passing the Buck

Charlene *Russell is frustrated by the lack of help that is being offered to Brenda, a girl in her first-grade classroom who has already been retained twice. She feels like everyone in school is passing the buck.*

"Hi, Ms. Russell!" Brenda shyly whispers to me on her way into the classroom. I noticed Brenda the first day I entered Ms. Leonard's class. She is an eight-year-old girl who has been left back twice in first grade and is on the verge of being left back again if something isn't done. Brenda is one of 28 children in our crowded urban classroom. Like most of the children, she comes from a very low-income family in a tough part of the city. Brenda is small for being almost nine years old. She converses easily with the other children, though at times she seems to talk about one thing while her classmates talk about something totally different.

During language arts, she often raises her hand to read but cannot actually decode the words. The words she does know are memorized and are very simple: *my, mom, Brenda, I, dog,* and so on. Her writing is unintelligible. Neither the cooperating teacher nor I can understand it without a translation from Brenda, and many times she doesn't know what she has written. She reinvents her own thoughts and writing as she shares her journal with us. For example, one day Brenda proudly showed me her journal, "Ms. Russell, come look what I wrote!" On the page was the following, "Itme yat is yofliofiy or. Wiy todty Itmey athe is yafliofiofy."

"Can you read this for me?" I asked Brenda.

She hesitated. Then, in a voice that sounded like she was reading, she said, "I will spend time with my Aunt Jackie and also my brother and my sister."

During one of our prep periods, I asked Ms. Leonard, "What else do you know about Brenda's family?"

She gave me some family history, which included a significant amount of mild mental retardation along with abuse. She also told me, "Brenda has not been able to make the connections between symbol-letter-word, which is preventing her further progress in school." That's certainly true. The only words Brenda knows are memorized. To compensate for her disability, she has learned to look at her classmates' work and copy, sometimes word for word, to be able to complete her work.

Another important thing I observed was that my cooperating teacher didn't seem to feel that Brenda's self-esteem was being affected negatively by her classmates throughout the academic sessions of the day. Six-year-old children are very candid and will not hesitate to let you know what's right and what's not. Unfortunately, this is the case for Brenda in Ms. Leonard's class. The students regularly let Brenda know when she isn't correct and have little tolerance for her struggle to learn new things. Because Brenda has little peer support, her own confidence and belief in herself have slowly deteriorated.

For her part, Ms. Leonard completed a 10-page application for the child study team to have Brenda tested. "When will they be able to test her?" I asked Ms. Leonard.

She sadly responded, "Probably not until October at the earliest."

I asked, "Is there something we could do in the meantime to help her?"

Ms. Leonard shrugged and replied, "Well, she'll get 45 minutes of help from the basic skills teacher once a week. Other than that, there's nothing we can do. It's up to the school."

As a fellow teacher, I totally disagree with my cooperating teacher. Brenda needs to feel that she is a vital and important part of the classroom, and it's our job to make sure that she does. Let's stop passing the buck!

Questions

1. What are the many issues that need to be considered in this case? Which do you think is the most important issue to focus on immediately? In the long term?
2. Do you believe that self-esteem is important for students' learning? What do you know about educational psychology that supports your view? What can Ms. Russell or Ms. Leonard do to help Brenda's self-esteem?
3. What role should Brenda's family play in her schooling? This case does not mention any contact with parents. What plan would you recommend?
4. Have you experienced any of Ms. Russell's frustration with passing the buck when children need extra support? In what ways have your experiences been similar to this case? How have your experiences been different from it?
5. What courses of action does Ms. Russell have to choose from in helping Brenda academically? Check with someone with a background in special education for his or her perspective of this case.

CASE 45

Worried About Tommy

Diana *Bartlett first notices a suspicious bruise on Tommy's face, then discovers other disturbing evidence of child abuse. She has been planning to have the second-grade class role-play resolutions to family conflicts as part of their social studies unit. She questions whether to let Tommy participate or to cancel the activity.*

I absolutely love the teaching environment I'm in. Ms. Galacey, my cooperating teacher, is very enthusiastic and has made my days at Orange Valley Elementary School nothing less than pleasurable. She never hesitates to share her ideas or insights with me. I believe that after three weeks we have developed a positive teacher–student relationship already.

One Monday morning, Ms. Galacey decided to let me have full control of the teaching experience in her classroom. I happily awaited the second graders to begin our day. Tommy, a very independent and mature second-grade student, entered the room. "Good morning, Tommy. How was your weekend?" I said enthusiastically.

"You know, Miss Bartlett, it's my birthday in one week, and I ain't getting a party or presents or anything," he responded with disappointment in his voice.

I suddenly found myself thinking about turning eight years old and of all the birthday parties I was given. But before I could think any further, Jamie, Richie, and José entered the classroom. Evidently these students had heard Tommy's bad news. However, the topic of birthdays and presents became suddenly joyful rather than sorrowful like Tommy's.

I could see how hurt Tommy was by the other children's birthday party stories, so I told Ms. Galacey about the problem when she entered the room. She said, "You know, it's not really uncommon for a child to say stuff like that in this school." She turned her attention to the children and said, "Everyone settle down now. It's time for us to discuss our theme of the month: Families, Friends, and Neighborhoods."

As I looked around the classroom, I saw each team eagerly discussing our theme. Tommy, however, just listened to the other students on his team. This was unlike him. "He is usually a leader," I thought to myself. Just then, I noticed a mark on his lower jaw. It was a bruise. I told Ms. Galacey what I had seen, and she called Tommy outside to the hall to speak to him about it.

When Ms. Galacey asked Tommy what had happened, he defensively said, "Nothing. I just bumped into a dresser in my room." She asked more open-ended questions, hoping to get more responses from Tommy, but that's all he kept saying. He then went back to his team where once again he just sat quietly.

The day progressed; it was almost time for art class. During the morning session, we had managed to go over our challenging work for the day. I had chosen to model Ms. Galacey's classroom structure by introducing all of the work for the day and then allowing students to choose the work they would like to complete first, second, third, and so on. I felt that this was very resourceful, especially for me today. Tommy completed his work silently. Once again I thought, "This just isn't Tommy."

During art class, I had the chance to speak with Ms. Galacey again about my observations and concerns. I knew that I could get some type of advice and guidance from her on how to handle this situation. She told me that Tommy's bruise would be documented along with his story about the bruise. I reminded her of his birthday party story, and she said she would document that as well.

I also asked her what I should do about an activity I had planned for this afternoon. I wanted to have the students role-play a family conflict and work on resolutions. But how could I expect Tommy to participate with all his pent-up anger? How could I let him not participate without having the other children question why he got to sit out? And what could I do if Tommy did role-play and responded in a manner that might be frightening to the children? Ms. Galacey answered, "Diana, it's your decision. You'll do the right thing. You have until 1:30 to make a decision. Whatever you decide will be fine with me."

After speaking with Ms. Galacey, I thought more and more about what to do. I don't know what bothered me more—having to make a decision or thinking about Tommy's experiences. I made a temporary choice to buy more time. I had the students work on a letter to their parents for open house. The students were going to write about what they were learning in school and leave it on their desks for open house night on Thursday.

Tommy chose to draw a picture for his mother before he wrote his letter. When I looked over his desk to see his picture, he said, "I'm gonna rip this up. I can't bring it home. Mommy will say it's an ugly mess, and she'll just rip it up for me." My heart began to sink deeper and deeper. I told him that it was a beautiful picture and that he should take pride in his work because he is an excellent student. I also told him I would be here for him if he needed to talk to someone about his feelings. He tried to smile as he thanked me, but I knew he wasn't ready to talk.

As I walked around, I observed the other children writing their letters and working on pictures like Tommy had done. Even when the going got tough for Tommy, he still managed to have the other students follow him. When I looked over at Tommy, I noticed that his pencil was moving. He was pressing it down on the paper as if he were carving letters into a tree. I could see the anger in his face, and I knew he needed to express his feelings.

I let the students work in the learning centers when they had finished their letters. This allowed me time to look at their letters and think about Tommy and the role-playing activity. When I got to Tommy's letter, I cringed:

Dear Mom,

Please don't be mad at me. I'll be a good boy. I promise I'll be a good boy. Just don't get mad at me.

Tommy

Thoughts ran through my mind. How do I help this child? What can I do for him? Why does a child have to deal with these things? I then showed Ms. Galacey the letter. She said, "We need to make a copy of this, and we have to continue documenting everything that he tells us or we see." It was then that I found out that Tommy was absent from school last year 39 times but was allowed to be promoted to second grade. Ms. Galacey told me that a social worker visits his family regularly.

After I received this information, I felt even worse about the situation than I had before. As I contemplated one last time what to do about the role-playing activity, I thought, "How am I going to walk away from this child in December?"

I knew I had to get the students focused on our activity. But what about Tommy?

Questions

1. What are the laws about reporting suspected child abuse in your state? What are your legal responsibilities as a teacher?
2. How can you best help a child like Tommy in your class? What other professionals are available for help?
3. What should Diana do now about the role-playing activity? Are there other activities or topics that Diana, or any teacher, should be especially sensitive about?
4. What do you think is Ms. Galacey's perspective on the problem? Why do you think she left the decision up to Diana?
5. What other information would you like to know about Tommy? Explain.

CASE 46

Too Much Love?

Charles *is an eight-year-old who has captured the heart of his student teacher, Debra Nichols. She wonders whether she loves him and the other students too much.*

I love these kids! Especially Charles. That in a nutshell is my problem. In September, I was placed in the Dawson School, a public elementary school located in one of the hottest drug spots in town. When I did a drive-by before my student teaching began, I thought to myself, "What am I doing in a place like this?" There was graffiti on almost every available spot on the building. The array of colors ranged from red, green, blue, and black to silver. I was scared. There were huge monster gates that protected all entrances of the building and security guards on every corner with walkie-talkies. What was I to think?

On my first actual visit, I was pleasantly shocked. With caution, I had entered the building, and my eyes were amazed. This was the most beautiful school I had ever seen. There were paintings, posters, glittering construction paper, and writings filling every wall. These works of art were done by what I would soon find to be the most wonderful students, the children of Dawson School. I knew at that moment that I was in the right spot. I took my coat off and took a deep breath. This was going to be an experience and a half.

Right away, Charles, an eight-year-old African-American boy, stood out for me. During my first encounter with him, I knew there was something special about this child. I could tell he was really smart, even though he wasn't doing well in school. Myra, my cooperating teacher, filled me in on his family history. His mother was a drug addict who has been in rehab several times. From there on in, I knew that Charles was going to be my little pal.

Then came the day that I was to actually teach the class. Parking my red Honda Civic outside near the playground, I saw some familiar faces. Someone, I'm not really sure who, opened the door to let me walk through the blue-painted hallway to the other side. There's the spot! A zillion teeny, tiny white teeth and happy smiling faces greeted me with, "Hi, Ms. Nichols." It was the best feeling in the whole entire world.

We as a class ventured up the stairs, chatting a bit about our weekends. We caught up on times lost. Then the moment arrived: time to be the teacher. Things changed except for my indescribable feelings. The lesson went just fine, but I found that it was hard to maintain any distance from the students. I want to be their friend, and at times I know I can't. Those are some of the hardest feelings to overcome. I am not sure if I do the right or wrong things. I feel as though I always need to be supporting their every move, and it can't be that way all the time.

Day after day, little dirty and clean hands are thrown high up in the air and many loud and soft voices sound, "Eww, eww, eww! Ms. Nichols, Ms. Nichols!" Do I have enough time to hear every story? Do I have time to answer each question? Maybe if it were my own classroom I would, but it's not, and time does not allow. But there are those extra special students who do need the undivided attention, and that is where I fit in.

For example, I want Charles to pass the second grade, and with my help I *know* he can do it. Every day, I keep a close watch on him to make sure that he is on top of his assignments. In a sense, I know I'm favoring him but not directly. Sometimes it's so hard. I only wish someone would have warned me about the attachment a teacher can have to a student. No, I am not trying to be his mother, but I am trying to push Charles in the right direction. I am so afraid that if I don't do this, no one will. Why should someone as brilliant and creative as Charles suffer or be retained because his home life is hard? But should I be so close to him? I don't know how to let go and allow him to make his own decisions. He is only an eight-year-old child who is still growing and learning. Sometimes I wonder if I am doing the right thing by being so emotionally involved with the students in this class. What can I say? I love these kids. Help!

Questions

1. Make a list of the pros and cons of becoming emotionally close to students. How do you feel about this in terms of your own teaching experiences?
2. Do you think a teacher can love too much? Explain your reasons.
3. Think back to your own educational past. What teachers stand out for you? To what extent did your favorite teachers show they cared for you? To what extent did they maintain a professional distance?
4. Would the issues in this case change if the students were older? Is it appropriate to be close friends with a student in high school? Middle school?
5. Is it natural to favor some students? What should a teacher do who likes some students more than others? What does it mean to have a professional relationship?

CASE 47

My Students, My Children

Francesca Molino is having a difficult time student teaching in a third grade in an inner-city school in which most of the children are very poor. She is upset about the living conditions that the children are faced with. She begins to buy them needed food and supplies and questions where she should draw the line between being a mother and being a teacher.

My internship was off to a great start. The children loved me, and I loved them. The teacher and I hit it off. We worked well at achieving goals together in the classroom. I quickly learned the students' names and something about each one. This is when I began to have trouble. I found out that roughly 85 percent of them were living in poverty. The entire school population is eligible for free or reduced lunch. I was horrified. I guess I was a little ignorant of other people's situations. I've lived in this city all my life but forgot that not everyone goes home to a warm house full of love and support. Soon I realized that these students were more unfortunate than I had thought. Some of their faces always seemed so sad.

Some students came in wearing the same clothes for a week. Others would come in without socks on. No pencils, crayons, scissors, or glue. Some without breakfast, lunch, or a snack. My heart bled every day. I found myself becoming upset about their lives. I even found myself thinking about them at night and over the weekend. There were a few particular students who really touched me. I noticed that they were extremely bright students, but their home life and economic status hindered them from working to their potential. Some of my students couldn't even complete their homework because they had no glue, scissors, or crayons at home.

Donald, a bright boy who loved math and writing, really made me start thinking. I knew it bothered him to not have his own school supplies. So one day I brought in a brand-new pack of crayons and pencils for him. I thought to myself, "Am I crazy? I can't keep doing this. Is this appropriate?" It broke my heart because I could tell that something was bothering Donald every day. I constantly had the unbelievable urge to go over and hug him. It killed me to know that I really couldn't. One morning he told me he'd found a rat in his toilet bowl. It was alive, and he was afraid. What could I say to him? How could I comfort him?

One day I noticed that Donald was particularly quiet and couldn't seem to concentrate on his seatwork. I approached him and said, "You look very sad. Is there something I can help you with?" He looked up at me with these big watery eyes and told me he hadn't eaten lunch. I became so upset that I wanted to go to the deli right then and there and didn't care about anything else. So when I went to move my car because of street cleaning, I brought him a bag of pretzels that was in my car. On another day, he told me his stomach hurt because he didn't eat breakfast.

I was becoming too attached to these children, particularly Donald. I wanted to bring in so many supplies, food, and clothes for him, but I knew that many of these children were in the same situation that he was. Could I bring in breakfast and snacks just for him? He made me wonder. By the beginning of November he had already come to school without his book bag three times. Once he couldn't bring his books to school because his baby brother had thrown his books into the toilet bowl and they had to dry. Isn't there any child supervision at home?

I could barely afford to put gas in my car, yet I wanted to buy these kids everything. Should a teacher provide these things for students? When does a teacher draw the line? What does a teacher do when her students' basic needs are not being met? How do I leave these kids in December? How can I separate being a mother and a teacher? Will my attachments to children like Donald conflict with my role as a teacher?

Questions

1. How do you personally relate to this case? What do you think is the line between mothering and teaching? How would your answer change based on the age of the students?
2. What can you do as a teacher to help students who do not have an environment at home conducive to learning? What role should the school as an institution play?
3. What expectations for homework can you have for children who are faced with the living conditions described in this case? Should children be punished for not doing their homework or given zeros for grades? How can you as a teacher make homework equitable for all socioeconomic levels?
4. How can Maslow's hierarchy of needs help us understand the issues in this case?
5. Have you ever purchased something for the classroom with your own money, or do you know of teachers who do? How common is this at your school? How do you feel about it? What can you do to get needed materials that the school doesn't provide? What other sources can you go to?

Case 48

On My Nerves

Jean Alston is challenged by Rosita, a sixth grader who always seems to be causing problems with her behavior. How can Ms. Alston keep a professional attitude when this student just gets on her nerves?

"Rosita, please sit down!" I heard myself screaming for the first time since my student teaching began.

"Rosita is bothering me!" David said.

"She doesn't listen!" Joshua complained.

"Ms. Alston, may I sharpen my pencil?" This was Rosita's repeated question of the day, made after walking all over the classroom and sharpening her pencil three times previously. In this sixth-grade classroom in which I am student teaching, the students sharpen their pencils at various times during the day; it is understandable. Almost everyone in the class understands that students cannot just get up and walk to the pencil sharpener, especially during a lesson, because it is disruptive to everyone else. Almost everyone understands, that is, except for Rosita.

The pencil-sharpening incident is just one example of her disruptive behavior. I have tried many things with this student. If I am in the middle of a lesson and she gets up, I will simply walk her back to her seat, quietly, without causing a commotion. If she is bothering other students, I will try to explain to Rosita that it is not right or fair for her to be doing this to everyone else. So far, however, nothing seems to work because she keeps doing the same thing.

I read with three different literature circles in class. Whenever it's time for Rosita's group to meet, she will begin to bang her hands on the book or make loud sounds. I continue reading and discussing the text with the rest of the students, trying to ignore her, but then she begins playing with the pages of the book and talking while other children are talking. I've tried to get her to see that the other students are as bothered by this as I am, but she keeps on behaving the same way.

Some days she is so disruptive that I just have to ask her to please return to her seat and leave the group. This does not seem to affect her in any way because in less than two minutes she will stand in front of everyone and just start asking continuously if she can go to the bathroom or some other request.

I have incorporated minilessons on behaviors into the social studies lesson I've been doing. I did not want to point out anyone in the class, especially Rosita. For example, I focused the discussion on manners, giving the students an example: "Would you like to have people talking, laughing, getting up, or walking around while you are reading or talking?" The students responded with enthusiasm, and very openly talked about how they felt when others were rude, using examples of recent events. I was impressed with the maturity shown by the group. After this lesson the other students' behavior, especially toward other people, has improved, but not Rosita's.

Some days I feel sorry for her because no one wants to be her friend or even sit by her. I try to justify and understand her behavior when she starts acting up, but I have to admit that she just really gets on my nerves. I find it hard to admit, especially in writing, that I just don't like Rosita. The whole class would be so much easier to manage without her. I am struggling to find my professional composure and treat her in an appropriate way, but I don't know what way that is!

Questions

1. What is Jean's ethical responsibility in this case? Can you give examples of when you felt the way that Jean does here?
2. How do you feel about Jean's attempts to manage Rosita's behavior so far? Do you think her actions have made sense?
3. Are there any other issues besides classroom management that need to be examined in order to help Rosita? What else would you want to know about her? About the curriculum? The other students?
4. Retell this case from Rosita's point of view. What do you imagine she is thinking?
5. How would looking at Erikson's stages of emotional development help a teacher to understand Rosita's needs and the classroom dynamics?

CASE 49

These Kids'll Steal Anything

Helen *Pulaski catches an eighth-grade student from the classroom next door stealing from her. She has to decide whether to turn in the student to be harshly punished or to cover for her.*

I sat in my car counting the minutes to begin my new and exciting experience of student teaching. Since the school had not asked me to come in for an interview, I didn't know what to expect. Although this urban K–8 school was not what I had requested, I knew I would love it since my junior practicum had gone so well.

Upon entering the antiquated-looking building, I began to realize this would be nothing like the model school I had done my junior practicum in. As the days went by, I confirmed that this school was quite the contrary. The principal was rarely in the school since he held other official positions. As a result, the power-hungry vice-principal was usually in charge. None of the staff seemed to get along with him. Although teachers pretended to like him, hypocritical comments raced through the faculty lounge. Obviously, this made for much tension within the school. Perhaps this was the reason for Ms. Anderson's demeanor. The first thing she said after meeting me was, "Helen, keep your purse with you at all times; these kids'll steal anything!"

Ms. Anderson had been teaching for 14 years and was convinced that one could not be a teacher and a friend. "You need to be much firmer with them; that is the only way they'll ever give you any respect." I, on the other hand, wanted to make friends with the students. The eighth graders that I was assigned to were on the brink of adulthood, and I felt that if they saw me as an equal who respected them, they would be more willing to open themselves up to me and in turn respect me.

I also wanted to incorporate different techniques I had learned about in college such as active listening and cooperative learning groups. Ms. Anderson didn't find these ways helpful. "Bringing yourself down to a student's level gives the students the opportunity to feel power, and you will lose yours." When I first asked about cooperative learning, Ms. Anderson immediately cut in, saying, "Sure those videos they show in college are all fine and dandy, but in the real world, Helen, the children get out of hand. Besides, cooperative groups don't work for all children."

Still, I saw that these students had to be given credit for their work. So when marking papers I decided to write comments on them other than "great" and "good job." I had to find what each child did well, not just what he or she did poorly. Despite the fact that writing comments took a little longer, the students were very happy, and I was quite pleased with myself. I was especially thrilled when Mossad, a shy boy who usually gets failing grades, came up to me and said, "Could you really tell I took my time? Because I did, and without anyone's help!" When I shared this with Ms. Anderson, she commented, "It must have taken you a lot of time to grade papers that way. The reason I don't do it is because as the classroom teacher, I'm just too busy."

Throughout this time, I had gotten to know well some of the students in the other classes. I had become particularly close to Pamela, a 12-year-old girl who was placed in a self-contained special ed. class next door. Pamela had many problems. Both her parents had recently died of AIDS, and she was presently living with her crazed grandmother and her aunt and uncle who beat her. I felt sorry for her, and I would try to pass by her class whenever I could to say hi.

I seemed to feel closer to the students than I was to the faculty. I even stopped eating lunch in the faculty lounge because their cynical comments bothered me so much. One day while returning from the pizzeria to have lunch in the classroom, I opened the classroom door only to find someone going through my bag. It was Pamela. My stomach turned. I couldn't say anything because the words wouldn't come out. The day before, someone had taken five dollars from the teacher's desk, and two weeks before that someone had taken 43 dollars from the classroom next door. Could Pamela have taken that money, too? So many things raced through my mind. "Why would she steal from me? I thought I was her friend," I said to myself.

Pamela threw herself on the ground. "Please," she begged. "All I wanted was a little lunch money. I swear I'll never do it again. This is the first time I've ever done anything like this. Please don't suspend me, please."

I wanted to be passionate, but my anger stepped in the way. "Just get out, and I don't want to see you around here again!" I snapped.

As Pamela left crying, I reflected on what I had done. How could I have said that to that poor girl? "Well, I know one thing. I am not going to tell anyone," I thought. "Who knows what these people would do to her!" When lunch was over, Ms. Anderson and the children rushed into the room. As I started getting ready for the next lesson, I heard a voice from the back of the room yell, "Who's been going through my things? Someone has left my drawers wide open, and I want to know who it was! Helen, was it you?" My jaw dropped. What was I going to do? If I took the blame, I might get into a lot of trouble, but if I told the truth, Pamela might get suspended.

Questions

1. What are the perspectives of the other people in this case? Retell the case from Pamela's viewpoint and from Ms. Anderson's. Does this change the way in which you interpret the events?
2. Try to use Kohlberg's theory of moral development to explain Helen's, Pamela's, and Ms. Anderson's reasoning. Which comes closest to your own reasoning?
3. What possible actions can be taken in this case by Helen and Ms. Anderson? What are the short-term and long-term implications of each action?

4. Why do you think Pamela was stealing? Have you had similar incidences in your own experiences as a teacher or as a student? How did these incidences compare with Helen's? What role do you think social class plays in this case?

5. How much do you think the role of school climate, such as Helen describes here, affects what happens in individual classrooms? What examples can you give to support your conclusions?

CASE 50

A Tough Decision

Carrie *Mills receives her first student teaching assignment in a working-class high school and is asked by her cooperating teacher to photocopy copyrighted materials that the school cannot afford to purchase.*

I was pleasantly surprised when I received my first student teaching placement at Adams High School. A large secondary school located near the waterfront, the school has an excellent reputation despite serious state-funding cutbacks. While I had read about these financial difficulties in the local newspapers, little did I suspect how personally this situation would affect me.

I had been working with my cooperating teacher, Ms. Johnson, for 10 weeks. She seemed to have it all together. I considered myself in a teaching partnership, and we had a good class. Making up the class were 24 students from blue-collar families who, for the most part, seemed to take Sequential II (10th-grade math) seriously. I had a strong rapport with the students and considered myself a champion of their best interests.

The teachers in the cafeteria had just about accepted me as one of their own. The student teaching experience was working out far better than I had hoped. There were generalized discussions about the number of math openings for the following semester and how recommendations from those teachers I worked and lunched with could help me land a job.

During that very afternoon, though, my bubble burst. It was then that my cooperating teacher handed me a math workbook and casually asked me to make 24 copies of pages 17 through 27 for the class. As I stood waiting for my turn at the school copier, I realized with a sudden lurch in my stomach that the material was clearly copyrighted.

I was in a real pickle. I asked myself, "What do I do now? Do I jeopardize my good relationship with my cooperating teacher by refusing to copy this material? Do I put my seemingly certain future employment at risk? Do I deny the students in my class valuable materials that they need to know and that students in other, more affluent school districts certainly have but that this school district definitely can't afford?"

At the same time I asked myself, "How can I break the law and make the copies? How widespread is copyright infringement? Are other laws being violated by the teacher or the school district? Will I be asked to break additional laws? What are the penalties if I'm somehow caught? Am I making a mountain out of a molehill?" I found myself staring at a now available photocopying machine, wondering.

Questions

1. Do you think Carrie is making a mountain out of a molehill? Do you think that this is a significant issue in teaching?
2. What responsibility do you think Carrie has to follow her moral and legal convictions in this case? What advice would you offer her? What experiences have you had in your student teaching with copying materials?
3. How well do you know copyright laws? What are you allowed to legally copy for educational use?
4. Have you found that you are lacking important teaching materials in your classroom? How do teachers improvise or obtain needed materials?
5. Have there been any times during your student teaching when you've been asked to do something that you were uncomfortable with ethically or that you strongly disagreed with? How did you handle such a situation?

CASE 51

Too Close for Comfort

Julio, a student teacher in high school social studies, has been privately help-ing one of his female students after school. He feels he is making great progress, but his cooperating teacher believes that Julio's meeting alone with the student is inappropriate. Julio questions whether this is such a serious problem and wonders how he can continue to help her.

During this student teaching experience, I've learned a lot more than just how to teach high school social studies. I never realized there were so many other things to worry about than just lesson plans and assessment.

My student teaching has been somewhat rocky. I've had some great days and even weeks when my lessons go well, the students behave, and I feel like I've accom-plished quite a bit. On other days, nothing seems to go right. Sometimes my lessons seem to be lost on the students, and I'm still struggling to keep them all on task with-out just lecturing at them. The one aspect of teaching that I've been more sure of is my relationship with the students.

I grew up in this town and at age 23, I'm only a little bit older than some of the students. The drop out rate in this school is pretty high; the kids just don't understand how important it is to stay in school. I feel like I can relate to their interests and con-cerns better than some of the older teachers. So many of the teachers seem to create a barrier between themselves and the students. I guess this helps them maintain their authority, but I went into teaching because I want to really help the kids and be a role model for them, not just teach content.

I've been pleased that one group of students has shown a real interest in my 11th-grade U.S. history class. They are working on a group project as part of their midterm grade and often come to me for extra resources or questions. A couple of days a week they usually hang out in my room at the end of the day, and we sit and talk about everyday things. Sometimes I also see them during lunch, and we share a joke or two.

One of the girls in this group, Sheila, has also stopped by to see me a few times for advice. At 16, she's got real problems with her family, and I think she just needs someone to listen. She lives in a really tough neighborhood. Her mom is on drugs and doesn't always come home at night, so Sheila takes on the responsibility of car-ing for her 12-year-old brother. She's often late to homeroom and rarely has any homework done. She also has just broken up with her boyfriend, and it seems her other friends sometimes get tired of her complaining.

I think Sheila has real potential though. I can tell from class discussions that she is very bright, but she doesn't apply herself at all to schoolwork. Her low self-esteem prevents her from taking any risks and trying new things academically. I'm trying to get her to see herself in a more positive way, both through our discussions and through feedback on her class assignments. In the last two weeks, she has actually handed in two very well-written papers. I feel that, given a little more time, I can really make a difference in her life, both personally and academically.

Unfortunately, my cooperating teacher, Mr. Blackmore, doesn't think so. The problem is that Mr. Blackmore coaches soccer and needs to leave right away at the end of the day. Sheila usually stops by right after school, so that means we are usually alone in the classroom. Mr. Blackmore feels that this situation is a serious problem. He is really worried about the possibility for what he calls "inappropriate contact." Evidently a few of the faculty members have noticed us together and have given him warnings about it. Yesterday he told me, "You are not only risking an uncomfortable situation, you are risking getting a future job in the school and possibly the district. It just isn't worth it."

I'm just having trouble believing it is that serious a problem. How are we as teachers supposed to reach out and help students when we have to be so worried about "how it looks" or what people will think? I feel like I am being penalized because there are so many weirdos out there who do act inappropriately. How can I work with this level of paranoia? Can I never be alone with a female student? Should I not talk to female students personally in the hall or lunch, but only in class? Does this mean I can't have a caring relationship with any of them?

And what am I going to do about Sheila? She has just begun to trust me and has shown so much academic improvement. If I tell her now that I can't meet with her after school anymore, how will she take it? I'm afraid she'll think that one more person has abandoned her.

Questions

1. Do you agree with Mr. Blackmore that this situation is a serious problem? Should Julio be allowed to be alone with a female student?
2. What are some of the behaviors that you think teachers do need to be concerned about? What are the policies at the school where you are student teaching?
3. How important do you think it is to have a personal relationship with students in high school? How about at other grade levels? Should teachers ever become friends with their students or socialize with them?
4. What options does Julio have? What advice can you give him for continuing to help Sheila while still following his cooperating teacher's mandate?
5. What other ideas can you think of to help Sheila improve her academic performance? What other professionals could help with her personal problems?

Case 52

Cheating on Exams

> **Debbie** *believes that the statewide tests given to her lower achieving high school math students are unfair. She notices a couple of the other teachers "helping" the students on the statewide standardized tests. She wonders where one draws the line between helping and cheating and what is most fair to the students.*

I've been teaching math for nine weeks in Kennedy High School, and I have finally gotten a handle on my five preparations each day. My cooperating teacher, Mr. Sykes, has been helpful with ideas, encouragement, and support. The best part of this experience has been the freedom Mr. Sykes has given me to try my own ideas, take responsibility, and learn from my mistakes.

I was especially pleased with the changes I had been seeing in my "slower" 10th-grade algebra classes. The students in these two algebra classes had such a defeatist attitude that I had spent weeks just trying to get them interested and to believe in themselves. Now Mr. Sykes has had me helping them prepare for the state testing next week. The state has established new standards in all of the content areas and began statewide assessments two years ago. I've been worried about how they'll do because even though they have made great progress, I think the test will only show what they can't do yet.

Yesterday, we had our monthly faculty meeting with our principal, Mr. Devora. Most of the meeting focused on the procedures for the state tests. After explaining the scheduling and room assignments, Mr. Devora gave us what I'd call a pep talk about how important the tests are. He finished by saying, "As you know, the last two years our school math scores have gone down slightly each year. The district is putting all kinds of pressure on us. We have got to show some improvement this year. I don't care how you do it, but use any way you can to help your students do well on these tests. You know what I mean. We just don't have an option for not improving."

After everyone had left, Mr. Sykes and I walked back to our room. "What exactly was Mr. Devora talking about with the district putting pressure on us?" I asked.

"Well, the board of education has decided to start publishing all the scores by teacher for each school so parents and taxpayers can see who is doing well and who isn't. They're also considering ways to tie our pay to test scores, but I think that might be awhile in coming," Mr. Sykes explained.

"But that hardly seems fair. What about the teachers in Academy High School who get all the smartest kids? How can the board compare their scores to ours? And even in our school, how are we supposed to make such a difference when we start with kids who are so far behind? The teachers will be fighting to only teach the honors classes. Who will want to teach the kids who really need lots of support?" I complained.

"Yeah, that's one of the problems. Another problem is in putting so much emphasis on one test. It just doesn't give a realistic picture of how much the students have improved or what they can do in other contexts," Mr. Sykes added.

I thought about that for a moment and then got up the courage to ask, "What did Mr. Devora imply when he said we should help our students any way that we can? Did he mean what I think he meant?"

Mr. Sykes answered, "Well, it's not like he means anything unethical. It's just that when we know these tests don't always measure all our students can do, it's frustrating to watch them do poorly. A lot of the students don't even care. They leave half the answers blank. Sometimes we'll just point out to kids that they need to look over their papers or remind them to check their work."

I decided to let the matter drop. I had never actually administered the state tests, and because they were new tests since I'd been in high school, I really didn't know what to expect.

The next week I learned plenty when I helped two of the math teachers proctor the tests for our lower performing students. At various points during the tests, they would lean over and say something like, "Look again at number 23" or "Check your work carefully." One of the teachers made sure the information the students needed for a couple of questions was posted right on the board. And the other teacher sort of "lost track" of the time and gave the students 10 minutes more than the test booklet said.

I kept my mouth shut and just did what I needed to get through the week. But throughout the whole ordeal, I felt mixed emotions about what the teachers were doing. I know I've heard of teachers actually changing the answers on the exams, and none of the teachers did anything that serious, but I wonder where we draw the line. Isn't this sending the message to the students that cheating is okay?

On one side I can understand how the teachers rationalize this. They argue that because these tests are so unfair anyway, it doesn't really matter if we improve the scores a bit. But on the other side, I believe the old saying, "Two wrongs don't make a right." I think the teachers may be wrong.

I wonder what will happen if I run into this when I am the classroom teacher. What happens if I'm the one teacher in the department who doesn't go along with this? Especially since it could mean that my students might then do poorly on the tests while the other classes perform better.

Questions

1. What do you think about the argument that "since the tests are unfair, it doesn't matter if we improve the scores a bit"? Do you agree, or not? Explain.
2. Do you think standardized statewide testing is unfair? Why? Why not? What other arguments can you give besides those mentioned in the case?

3. Do you think students of all achievement levels should take the same tests? What adaptations should be allowed, if any?
4. What would you do if you felt that the tests were unfair? What options do teachers have when they disagree with school policies?
5. Do you think all the actions Debbie describes are "cheating"? Where would you draw the line between "cheating" and helping students demonstrate what they know?

For Further Reading

Damon, W. (1988). *The moral child.* New York: Free Press.

> This book covers empathy, shame, and guilt; learning about justice though sharing; culture, gender, and morality; the influence of family and peer group; and teaching values in schools. It is a scholarly summary of theory and research with a practical focus.

Educational Leadership, 54, 1997.

> This themed volume is a special issue on social and emotional learning. It presents 20 articles on emotional health, schools as communities, violence prevention, success in high school, reclaiming motivation, and other subjects addressing all grade levels.

Erikson, E. (1963). *Childhood and society* (2nd ed.). New York: Norton.
Kohlberg, L. (1963). The development of children's orientation toward a moral order. Part 1: Sequence in the development of moral thought. *Vita Humana,* 6, 11–33.

> These are the original publications of Erikson's and Kohlberg's theories. For a succinct review of these theories of personal, social, and emotional development, see Eggen, P., & Kauchak, D. (1997). *Educational psychology: Windows on classrooms* (3rd ed., pp. 76–103). Upper Saddle River, NJ: Merrill/Prentice Hall.

Lawton, T. (1997). Encouraging friendships among children. *Childhood Education: Infancy Through Adolescence,* 73, 228–231.

> This article examines research on loneliness and provides practical suggestions for friendship development and the role that adults can play in their relationship with children.

McCracken, J. (Ed.). (1986). *Reducing stress in children's lives.* Washington, DC: National Association for the Education of Young Children.

> This book compiles short articles by many authors that cover a huge range of topics related to stress and children. The book has a very practical focus based on theory and research.

Noddings, N. (1992). *The challenge to care in schools: An alternative approach to education.* New York: Teachers College Press

> This book addresses some of the issues facing our students in this day and age, such as school violence, substance abuse, and sexuality, from the perspective of curriculum and suggests how schools could address these issues based on the philosophy of caring. This is a good book for beginning the discussion of what role alternative views, such as caring, could have in our public schools.

Palmer, P. (1998). *The courage to teach: Exploring the inner landscape of a teacher's life.* San Francisco: Jossey-Bass.

> The premise of this work is that good teaching comes from the identity and the integrity of the teacher. Good teachers are able to weave a complex web of connections among themselves, their subjects, and their students, so that students can learn to weave a world for themselves. The author argues that good teaching is not in teachers' methods but in their hearts.

Slaby, R., Roedell, W., Arezzo, D., & Hendrix, K. (1995). *Early violence prevention: Tools for teachers of young children.* Washington, DC: National Association for the Education of Young Children.

This step-by-step guide for the teacher covers many areas of violence prevention that might not otherwise be considered. A thorough guide for early childhood and elementary teachers, it also has implications for teaching older children.

SECTION 6

Challenges of Working with Other Professionals

CASE 53

A Difference of Opinion

Mary Cosgrove faces a tough challenge when she is assigned bus duty by the principal and it interferes with her first-grade classroom work. This creates resentment on the part of her cooperating teacher, which comes to a head when they have a disagreement over how to handle a child who is not bringing in his homework.

I did my student teaching in a small, tree-lined suburban town that lies on the outskirts of a large metropolitan area. The majority of residents in the town are white, middle-class, single-family-home owners. The town has one high school, a middle school, and several elementary schools. I was given a first-grade classroom assignment and looked forward to the experience.

I was eager to enter the teaching profession. Since all of my previous work experience was confined to the business world, however, I worried about my ability to work with children in a group. As a single parent and head of a household, I also was extremely anxious due to the financial stress of surrendering my job in order to fulfill my student teaching requirement.

At an informal meeting prior to Labor Day, I met with my cooperating teacher, Regina Conners. Regina was a teaching professional with 18 years of experience in the primary grades. I was apprehensive as I handed Regina the written guidelines for my student teaching assignment.

"What are you required to do exactly?" Regina surprised me by asking.

I handed her a booklet that outlined the requirements, and we briefly discussed the nature of a first-grade classroom teaching assignment. Then we exchanged a few details about our personal lives, marital status, and children. I began to feel very comfortable with Regina when she shared, "I have two-year-old twin boys at home. I had to return to work the year after my maternity leave was over, and I'm not real happy about going back to work so soon."

I sympathized, saying, "I was in the same situation with my daughter, so I know just how you feel. Although you love being on the job, there's always that sense that you'd like to have more time with your children."

Regina added, "I'm also a little annoyed that the principal assigned me a student teacher both this semester and next. I just don't feel like I have the time or energy for the extra work this entails."

I, of course, felt terrible. Being new to the teachers' world, I hoped that I would be successful and not a burden on Regina. These concerns were compounded when Regina added, "The first-grade curriculum is extremely important. The children's learning future could be severely affected if it is not carried out properly." I felt compelled by these words to model my student teaching after Regina's teaching style.

The first few days of school were filled with excitement for me and the students in my classroom. I met the children, learned their names, and felt enthusiastic but timid about the prospect of teaching. Initially, Regina put me to work cutting paper and preparing supplies. I watched as she molded a cohesive group of first graders out of a classroom full of ex-kindergarten students by giving clear instructions about what was expected.

As the days went by, I continued to observe Regina's instruction and to assist with the manual preparations for lessons. During the second week of school, though, another responsibility was suddenly added to my duties that proved to be time-consuming, interfering with my classroom teaching and complicating my relations with my cooperating teacher: I was assigned to bus duty. Bus duty is not normally the job of the first-grade teacher. However, the principal of the school was short of financial resources and selected me to perform the task of meeting the school bus three times during the day—for 15 minutes at 12:30, 2:20, and 2:55.

The daily class interruptions caused by my bus duty irritated Regina, who felt that I should not be doing this task. I, on the other hand, had been instructed by my college program administrator to do whatever I was asked by the school. I did not feel that I could tell the principal that I was refusing bus duty, but I also worried when I realized the breach of camaraderie that the situation was creating between me and my cooperating teacher. As the weeks progressed, I noticed that I was not assuming more teaching tasks. I needed to talk more with Regina, I reflected, but there never seemed to be time in the day for this much needed communication.

The semester was passing by rapidly, and I was developing a severe problem in formulating concrete lessons for the first grade. My confidence was dropping sharply. Moreover, while I continued to try to model my teaching methods on those of my teacher, I did not agree with Regina's style of disciplining students. She was a strict authoritarian and a yeller, while I never liked that way of relating to children. The students were generally well behaved and easily motivated, so there usually were no problems in this area.

The tensions that had been developing between Regina and me came to a head when a disciplinary incident arose, and I did not handle it in the same way that my cooperating teacher would have. Richie, a student that Regina thought might have an attention deficit disorder, failed to return his homework one morning. I was aware that Richie was getting no help with his homework, even though a letter had been sent home requesting that his homework be checked each night by an adult. Thus, when I asked where the homework was and he stammered, "I did it, but I forgot it at home," I simply asked him to bring it when he returned after lunch.

I knew that Regina's policy for a missed homework assignment was to say in a disapproving tone, "That's a zero in my grade book," but I was concerned that Richie wasn't getting the help he needed at home. When I tried to explain my reasoning to Regina, she would not listen, insisting sharply, "You had better do it my way next time, or I'll step in and handle it myself." I wanted to discuss the issue further, but again there was no time.

The semester was eight weeks in, and I had not been encouraged to take over any more than the daily science and spelling lessons. I still had bus duty, which interfered with my work in the classroom and created resentment on the part of my cooperating teacher. And now I had a serious disagreement with Regina over how to relate to the children. How could I turn this situation around?

Questions

1. Write a few sentences about this case as though you were Mary, her cooperating teacher, and the principal. How does it help to view this situation from multiple perspectives?
2. To what extent did the disciplinary issue with Richie affect the relationship between Mary and her cooperating teacher? Discuss.
3. What should teachers do when students fail to hand in homework? To what extent does this reaction depend on the age of the student? What other factors influence the failure of students to turn in homework? Explain.
4. What are the possible causes of Mary's problems this semester?
5. What suggestions would you give Mary for improving the rest of her student teaching experience?

CASE 54

Student Teacher or Just Helper?

Katherine Berman tries hard to get her first-grade class to see her as the teacher, but she has difficulty getting them to respond to her the way they do to her cooperating teacher. Should she be their teacher or their friend?

I briefly met my cooperating teacher, Ms. Terrazzo, and her first-grade class two days before I began student teaching. The principal took me on a tour of the school, and I stopped in the classroom. The principal told the class, "Good morning, this is Miss Berman. She is going to be working in your class as a student teacher for the next few months."

I overheard one boy say, "Oh, yeah, she looks like a teacher. She's nice and all."

I was very flattered and thought, "This is going to be great. The children seem nice and excited to have a student teacher." My cooperating teacher, on the other hand, gave me mixed feelings. I decided I would go in with an open mind.

I caught on to the routine of the class quickly. The morning schedule included their specials, silent reading, rhyming, writing, and math. For the most part, the children responded to me in a positive way.

The first week, while my cooperating teacher would give a lesson, I would walk around to make sure the children were following her. If the children had any questions, they would ask me.

I was happy because I felt they saw me as a student teacher. However, I also felt I was a bother to my teacher. She made me feel welcome, but I just kept thinking that I was adding more work and pressure to her already-busy day. The school had recently changed its reading, language arts, and math curriculum significantly, moving toward more holistic instruction. This meant a lot of extra planning for Ms. Terrazzo as she struggled to learn new ways to teach and meet the demands of the school principal who had high expectations.

Whenever I was working with a child, I looked around to see if the teacher was watching. I constantly questioned my actions: Was that right? Should I have said that? I began to doubt myself, so I often asked Ms. Terrazzo, "Am I doing all right? Is there anything I should change?" She usually replied that I was fine and would start talking about things that she needed to change or work on. This really didn't help me. I realized that there was nothing I could do about it at the time. It wasn't my classroom.

One day Ms. Terrazzo was absent, so I thought, "This is a great opportunity for me. I'm free!" Well, it turned out to be a disaster. The children were off the wall. I was so frustrated because nothing I had learned was working with this class.

The next day Ms. Terrazzo returned, and the children were back to normal. I began to think I was doing something wrong.

One girl, Charlene, said to me that morning, "Miss Berman, you're my pal and my special friend!"

I quickly blurted out, "No, I'm your student teacher." Of course, I wanted her to feel that she was my friend, but I was concerned that the children didn't listen to me because they didn't see me as a real teacher.

The next day, I became very frustrated when I was working with Stephen one-on-one with a reading book. Mohammed was whining for me to help him, while Melissa and Diana pushed their papers in my face. This was all new to me, so I tried desperately to help them all. They must have sensed my frustration as I told them, "You're just going to have to wait a minute. I can't do everything and help you all at once!" The children backed away and slowly went back to their seats. I felt like I had blown my chance to help them in a positive way.

Later at group time, Ms. Terrazzo told them, "Kids, you have to remember that Miss Berman is not Superwoman. You have to give her a break and not all jump on her for help at once." I was somewhat embarrassed but at the same time felt relieved that she had mentioned it to them.

The next week, Ms. Terrazzo was absent again. This time I was very nervous. When the kids filed in at 8:30 and saw she wasn't there, they were immediately loud, unruly, and unresponsive to me. I decided it was time for a group talk. I gathered the students together on the rug for storytime and told them, "We really need to work together in this class, especially when Ms. Terrazzo isn't here. It makes me very sad when you all don't listen to me. Let's try to have a nice, calm day." Well, it didn't work. I had difficulty getting them to listen to me or follow the normal routine. They dawdled, played, talked, and ran around the class. Even the substitute had difficulty establishing any kind of order.

The next day, Ms. Terrazzo was back, and to my amazement, the children were well behaved and under control. Now I was sure I was doing something wrong. Later in the day, Nicholas began talking back to me when I reminded him it was time to put the silent reading books away. He looked up at me and sneered, "I know. I'm not deaf!"

I nearly fell over. I told him in my sternest voice, "That kind of talk is not appropriate and not nice. I don't want to hear it again." Well, of course, he repeated it to me various times throughout the day. I just began to ignore his response.

When I took the kids to specials, Sheila ran off down the hall. I called to her, "Walk, please, Sheila!" but she kept right on going. I ignored that, too. I decided to become their friend since they were just not seeing me as their teacher. I knew that went against everything I had learned. It would be great to be both teacher and friend if I could draw the line, but I had no line. What was I going to do when I had to take over the class completely in a couple of weeks?

Questions

1. Can you identify the problems Miss Berman is having? What do you think are the causes of those problems? List as many as possible.

2. What do you think is Ms. Terrazzo's view of the case? How would she describe the events? What could she do to make a difference?
3. How could parents have a role in this situation? In what ways can they be included to improve the situation?
4. What classroom management principles would you advise Miss Berman to consider?
5. What knowledge of child development should Miss Berman keep in mind to help her in this case?

CASE 55

How Am I Doing?

Jacob Roberts has serious doubts about his progress as a student teacher in a fifth-grade class because his cooperating teacher has given him no feedback. She has been aloof since the beginning of the semester, and he has not been able to develop a more positive relationship.

I waited in the parking lot on my first day. I watched as droves of students were piling into the large and ominous school building. For some reason the school seemed bigger than I remembered when I went to elementary school here. I watched the students move past my car. Occasionally someone would stop to look at me as I sat with my hands clenched tightly around the steering wheel.

"I can do this, I can do this," I thought, trying to reassure myself. "I have no choice but to do this. I've kind of put all of my eggs in this educational basket. I'd better go inside."

I then spotted a fellow student teacher walking toward the main staircase. "At least I won't have to go in by myself," I thought as I locked my car door. "Steve! Wait up!"

We walked together to the main office. We were instructed to wait in the library for an orientation given by one of the vice-principals. While in the library, Steve and I were greeted by fellow student teachers. The air was thick with nervousness and excitement. Everyone looked like eager professionals: shined shoes, pressed collars, and brand-new briefcases.

After the orientation we student teachers were assigned to our cooperating teachers. Steve and I were assigned to two teachers who shared a homeroom, and we noticed that the teachers were friends.

"I know your cooperating teacher," Steve said to me, peering at his assignment sheet.

"How is she?" I asked.

"She's nice, a little quiet. She mostly keeps to herself, but she's very nice," Steve replied.

We met our cooperating teachers and exchanged introductions. Steve's teacher was very warm and cordial, asking questions about his college career and his hobbies. My cooperating teacher asked me to sit down while she graded some papers. I sat in silence for several minutes, listening to Steve and his cooperating teacher talk about education and their personal lives.

Later that day, right before lunchtime, I saw Steve in the hall. "Where are you off to, Steve? You want to have lunch together?"

"Sorry, Jacob, I'm going out to lunch with my cooperating teacher. Wait a minute! I thought you were coming too. I mean, after all, your cooperating teacher is coming with us."

I felt a great lump form at the base of my throat. Why wasn't I invited? I tried to think about what I had done that could have turned off my cooperating teacher. It wasn't as if she blatantly hated me; she was nice. Or was she? I thought back to the first few periods of the day. She moved from lesson to lesson with little discussion. I thought it was kind of strange that there was an absence of small talk. Although I dislike the silly conversations people have when they first meet, I was concerned that absolutely nothing was being said between the two of us.

A few weeks later, when I began taking on more teaching responsibility, my confidence was further tested by her lack of input. Not only did she not give me any suggestions on how to manage the classes, but she didn't even talk about my lessons. Once in a while she would ask me to look at the plan book and roster, but besides that little else was discussed. I had no idea how I was doing as a teacher.

I began to get nervous. I was very confident about my teaching abilities. I was getting along quite well with my students. But the void that was created by my cooperating teacher grew into a dark monster of despair. Maybe she didn't like the way I was teaching? Maybe she didn't like me as a person? Maybe I wasn't a good teacher? I began to ask myself if I was doing the right thing. I knew that I desperately needed to talk to my cooperating teacher about my feelings, but I kept hesitating and putting it off because I didn't know how to begin.

Questions

1. What is the role of feedback in learning? Think of your own experiences in learning a new skill. How did you know you were on the right track?
2. What kind of feedback is the most helpful? What has helped you most in your student teaching?
3. Compare the effects of negative criticism and positive feedback that you have gotten. How have they affected your motivation?
4. How does this case relate to your teaching and the feedback you give your students?
5. How important is it to be friends with the cooperating teacher? What is the best kind of relationship to have? What possible options does Jacob have? How important is it to have positive relationships with coworkers? Why?

CASE 56

Stereotyping in the Teachers' Room

Sonya *Burke hears other teachers in the faculty lounge using stereotypes to label students, and she is afraid that their remarks will prejudice her relations with her fifth-grade students.*

My student teaching experience, which is taking place in an elementary school near my home in a small, close-knit community, is turning out to involve more than learning from and teaching my students; it also involves having to hear stereotyping and labeling. This doesn't occur in the classroom but in the teachers' room. This lounge with tables and chairs, a bathroom, a refrigerator, a soda machine, and a microwave is the common meeting place at our school. Teachers come together during lunchtime, it appears, just to speak negatively about their students:

"This one has a behavior problem."

"That one has an attitude."

"She talks too much and never pays attention."

These are some of the comments that are expressed in the teachers' room, where teachers compare notes about students and place labels on them.

Other than this problem, I am in an ideal situation. I love my fifth-grade class and have a terrific cooperating teacher, Ms. Barbieri, a recent graduate of the education program at my college. I count myself lucky because she uses the same constructivist, student-centered principles that I learned at school. Ms. Barbieri employs lots of group work, hands-on activities, and writing across the curriculum. She respects the learners, and they respect her. It is just wonderful to witness the children thrive in a setting I had previously heard about only theoretically. My student teaching is definitely showing me that active learning really works.

Outside my classroom, however, it is a whole different story. It is clear that many of the other teachers in this school do not respect the students in the way that Ms. Barbieri does. Too many times I find myself in the middle of all the discussions about students in the infamous teachers' room. I try to ignore the comments about children in my class, but despite my efforts, they stick in my mind. I believe strongly that each student deserves to start out each year with a clean slate. Yet while I'm teaching, the stereotypes remain in my head. "Maybe I should not call on him" or "I'd better not sit him with her" are some of the thoughts that run through my mind because of the comments that I hear while I'm in the teachers' room.

I believe that the gossiping affects not only teachers but also the students. They can sense how a teacher feels, especially how he or she feels about them personally. Students often find themselves locked into a role that they have played for so long they don't know how to get out of it. Students deserve the right to have an education.

They should not have to worry about what negative comments their teachers are saying about them. They should have to worry only about their academics.

I brought this situation to the attention of Ms. Barbieri. "The constant labeling and complaining in the teachers' room is getting to me," I told her. "It's affecting how I look at some of the students in our class."

"I know," she responded. "It bothers me, too, but you can never stop them. I learned that early on. The best you can do is to hang onto your ideals and try not to take what the others say too seriously. That's the best approach."

I also discussed the situation with my supervisor, Mr. Kramer. He basically said the same thing as Ms. Barbieri. He also told me that I was lucky to have the placement I have, and I certainly agree with him on that. "Just count your blessings that you have such a fantastic cooperating teacher and ignore the comments in the teachers' lounge," was his advice.

Well, I have tried to ignore them, but I can't. They are experienced teachers, and in many cases what they say is right on the mark. Some of the children that they complain about really do have problems. And sometimes I sense that the teachers are not being malicious when they talk about the children. Still I worry about what all this negative talk does to the students at this school, both inside and outside our classroom.

This whole situation has put me in a bind. Because of my opposition to the gossiping, backbiting, prejudice, and complaining, I am tempted not to go to the teachers' lounge any more. That way I won't be affected by their comments. But I don't want to seem like I'm not a team player. Already some of the teachers have made remarks about how quiet I am when I don't join in their talk. I don't want to let them know that I don't approve of what they do, and I'm afraid that if I don't continue to hang out in the teachers' room, they'll be offended. At the same time, I really don't like the way they stereotype certain students. What can I do?

Questions

1. Why, in your opinion, do the teachers' comments have such a strong effect on Sonya's own views of students? Have you experienced this labeling and stereotyping in your placement?
2. How might Sonya's situation be different if she were a member of the faculty of her school?
3. What are the student teacher's options in this case? What advice would you give her? Should she stay out of the teachers' room or continue to join the teachers?
4. What role does peer pressure and peer support play in teaching? How important is it to fit in and be a part of the conversation in the teachers' room?
5. Why do you think teachers label and stereotype children? What can you do to help children who are locked into negative roles?

CASE 57

Innovative Teacher or a Big Goof-Up?

Naomi Torres is mortified when her principal yells at her about a mistake with her sixth-grade class that was made by her cooperating teacher. She is hurt and angry that the cooperating teacher has let her take the rap, and she is worried that the principal now sees her as a big goof-up.

I have been placed in an elementary school in an urban town near my home. I'm in a difficult sixth-grade class. Yet I adore the students and at first had all kinds of ideas about activities I wanted to do with them. I thought if I could be really impressive, I could get a permanent job here since I had been told that this school was looking for innovative teachers.

When I first met my cooperating teacher, Ms. James, it seemed like a dream come true. I felt fortunate to have been placed with such an amicable person. Ms. James is easygoing and warm, and by the second week of class, I felt comfortable with the children, and Ms. James and I had established a rapport.

Most of the faculty in this school are pleasant. The principal, Mr. Cortez, met me on my first day, and I always make it a point to say hello whenever I see him in the hall. Sometimes he ignores me, and other times he offers me a thin smile. It doesn't bother me, though. I figure he has a lot on his mind, being the principal of 950 students and managing the faculty. Needless to say, I do like the school, and I'm more or less happy with the way my teaching is progressing.

My classroom, as I mentioned, is very active. I was surprised to find that the children need to be reprimanded constantly. In fact it's rare that even 20 minutes go by before either Ms. James or I have to raise our voices to gain control of the class. On my first day, Ms. James informed me that this was her worst class in her 29 years of teaching. I was disheartened to learn this because I always pictured my class as a smoothly functioning student-centered one with lots of small-group work and active learning projects.

Well, I woke up to reality real fast during my first week. This class is just how Ms. James described it and then some. I now understand why she always turns to bookwork instead of fun free centers and activities. I agree with her that these children are not able to work in groups without causing some kind of commotion. I can just imagine that someone would always be yelling and antagonizing others who really want to do the work. Things would soon start flying, chairs would be jostled, and children would freely roam around the room. As a result of this behavior, the focus of the entire class would be lost.

Anyway, I knew that I had my hands full, but I figured, "What am I here for? I thought if I could handle this class, then I could handle any class and establish my reputation throughout the school." I found it funny that whenever Ms. James introduced me as her student teacher, other faculty members gave me their sympathy, paid their condolences, and wished me good luck. I was beginning to almost feel as though I were interning in a funeral home.

It must have been the second or third week that I suffered my first, at least in my eyes, major setback. It was on a bright Thursday morning, a day like many others, when the principal, Mr. Cortez, yelled at me. I use this word purposefully because that's just what he did.

It happened like this. On every floor, the students eat lunch in their classrooms. At a certain point, every class is let out to get their lunches and bring them back to their class to eat. My class is the last on that floor, and they are not to be let out until 11:40. On this particular day, however, Ms. James dismissed the class about five minutes early. This class, being the loud, rowdy bunch that it is, never lined up but charged through the door and down the hall to pick up lunch trays.

Ms. James stood by the door and watched the students, shaking her head. Suddenly I heard a loud voice shout in the hall, and she turned to me and said, "Uh-oh! Here comes Mr. Cortez! They're not really supposed to be let out early." Then I was stunned when Ms. James casually walked into the room toward the back by the windows and stood behind the easel.

It all happened so fast. I was left standing right in front of the door, and as the children ran back into the classroom with their lunches, Mr. Cortez came in behind them. Probably because of where I was standing, I was the one he saw first. He looked directly at me and bellowed, "Ms. Torres, they cannot be let out to get lunch before 11:40! Lunch starts at 11:40. They need to be quiet and orderly when they walk down the halls!"

I stood there dumbly and murmured, "Okay," as if I didn't know when lunch starts. I was mortified. I felt like a child and was sure I had blown all chances of proving myself as a teacher. Mr. Cortez turned and left, and Ms. James came to the front of the room with her hand over her mouth, giggling. I call it giggling because that's what it seemed like to me. She just said, "Oooops!" I couldn't believe it! Tears sprang to my eyes, and all I kept saying was, "He yelled at me. He yelled at me."

Ms. James told me not to worry about Mr. Cortez, that it wasn't a big deal to him. Then she went to get her lunch. As much as I like her, I couldn't believe she cowered behind the easel and let him say that without coming forward to speak up. I was so hurt and surprised that she let me take the rap. After all, she is the classroom teacher, and it was she who dismissed the class. I was upset, thinking that Mr. Cortez probably believed that I had dismissed the students and that I hadn't even bothered to learn the class schedule. I wanted so badly to run after him and clear this matter up, but what if it really wasn't a big deal to him? I didn't want to get the reputation of being a person who tattles on my cooperating teacher, yet I was concerned about what he thought of me and my teaching.

A day later, I still don't know what to do. This morning when I saw Mr. Cortez, I said hello as though he had never yelled at me, even though I was burning with embarrassment. I'm angry at Ms. James for not taking responsibility for what happened. She doesn't even know how much this bothered me, and I'm perplexed about how to approach her, if at all. I had wanted to establish myself as an innovative teacher at this school, and already I'm feeling like I'm seen as one big goof-up.

Questions

1. What are some of the causes of Ms. Torres's problems?
2. How do you feel about Ms. James's labeling this class the worst ever? What effect has this had on the student teacher's actions? On the children's actions?
3. Do you think it is true that some classes need book work instead of student-centered activities? What ideas do you have for teaching students how to work in groups?
4. Retell this case from the perspective of Ms. James and the principal. Why do you think they reacted the way they did?
5. What can Ms. Torres do now? What is the best way for her to handle this dilemma?

Case 58

The Schedule Will Not Permit It

> **David** *is student teaching in a sixth-grade remedial reading class in a school in the midst of a labor action. Because the class is having trouble staying on task, David suggests changing the sixth-grade schedule to accommodate two half-hours instead of one continuous hour, but he is met with opposition.*

I am student teaching in an urban school district whose teachers are working without a contract. The union leaders decided upon a job action that is designed to draw attention to this labor problem. The teachers are adhering strictly to the previous contract as it relates to starting and ending times of the day, so they are not staying after school or doing any extra work. This has resulted in an actual or perceived lack of preparation time for the teachers in my school. Along with this loss of preparation time has come a sense of urgency during the school day to accomplish certain tasks. The teachers repeatedly complain about this job action but feel compelled to adhere to it because it was agreed to be in their best interest.

I am teaching the remedial reading group, which is required to meet for an hour each day. But nothing stipulates that it has to be a continuous hour. The on-task time of this group seems to top out at 20 minutes. I usually use the remaining 40 minutes to address behavior problems and try to refocus the students.

I politely suggested to my cooperating teacher, Mr. Warner, that the students might be better served if the reading class were rescheduled for two half-hour sessions. I pointed out, quite tactfully, that even when I was observing my cooperating teacher, I noticed that he was having difficulty keeping these students on task for an hour. Although he agreed with my observations and my suggestion, he said, "I think it would be too difficult to reschedule the classes. The other sixth-grade teachers are comfortable with the present schedule. I would feel uncomfortable suggesting a change in their daily schedule." Although I sensed that this was as far as I should go with this idea, I decided to bring up the schedule with the other two sixth-grade teachers.

The following day, I happened upon Ms. Hudson, one of the other teachers, at the copy machine in the library. When I brought up my concern about the remedial reading group, she agreed but said it would be too difficult to change the existing schedule. When the machine spit out her last copy, Ms. Hudson retrieved it and left. The conversation was over.

The schedule of all the teachers in the school was being disrupted to achieve a labor management agreement. I compared this disruption to the seemingly impossible chore of adjusting three sixth-grade teachers' schedules for the benefit of the remedial reading group. I'm sure these are dedicated teachers; I really believe they care about all their students, but they don't see the irony of this situation. In my view they acquiesced to a schedule change for the sake of money but not for the sake of the children.

If a schedule change could keep the students on task for 20 minutes out of each half-hour, we would double the on-task time of each reading student. This would go a long way toward bringing what is a chore for these students up to the level of enjoyment. But our schedules will not permit it.

Questions

1. Why do you think the students are unable to stay on task for more than 20 minutes? What do you think of David's suggestion that the schedule be changed to accommodate the remedial reading class? What are the disadvantages of having a shorter class?
2. What other suggestions for helping the remedial reading group can you come up with besides changing the schedule? What classroom management techniques or teaching methods would you recommend?
3. What do you think of the role of labor unions in teaching? How would you react as a teacher to the type of job action described in this case? What types of job actions, if any, do you think are necessary? Acceptable?
4. Have there been times during student teaching when you wanted to make suggestions that you thought would improve the students' learning experience? How did you handle this?
5. What is the role of a student teacher in making suggestions such as David's? Do you think that he overstepped his bounds?

CASE 59

Who's in Control?

Brian Niko, a student teacher in an eighth-grade English class, has philosophical differences with his cooperating teacher, who appears reluctant to allow him to take over the class.

My first encounter with my cooperating teacher, Ms. Collins, was a pleasant one. She was helpful and friendly enough. Obviously she knew a lot about teaching, having 20 years in the profession. I discovered all this when we met on the day I stopped in just to get oriented before the actual practice of teaching junior high English began. Things changed the first full day at the school.

The real problems started when I showed Ms. Collins some of the texts that we are currently using in our college workshops. She picked up my text on whole language, looked through it for a second or two, then threw it down on the table, saying to me, "This is doomed to fail and isn't workable in a real school setting." I knew then that there was a conflict in philosophies brewing here.

I explained, "I would just like the chance to try out some of these strategies in a real classroom setting."

She said, "Go ahead!" and then smiled. I could see she wasn't sincere.

When my college supervisor, Dr. Rugel, came to the school to meet Ms. Collins, all did not go well. Ms. Collins gave my supervisor a polite but cold reception. Dr. Rugel outlined what was expected of me on behalf of the college and explained that she espoused a whole language approach to teaching English. As I expected, once Dr. Rugel left, Ms. Collins had nothing but negative comments to make about her and her teaching ideas. I was very uncomfortable with this situation.

The next week, I was supposed to take over Ms. Collins's honors class, but every day she had a different excuse to put it off. We decided on procedures, group sizes, rules of participation, and the like; but when the day came to start, she stayed in the class with me and changed the rules without letting me know ahead of time. It became apparent to me that she needed to be in control and that she was reluctant to give up her classes to me.

Although I finally was given three classes to work with, for the first few days Ms. Collins found it necessary to stick around for a while, which I quite understood. What did throw me off, though, was that a few times she would leave, then come back under the pretense of having forgotten something, and then proceed to teach the lesson that was just begun. On one occasion, she completely got the class off on a tangent, then said, "Oh, I'm sorry to interrupt," and left the room, leaving me feeling unfocused and distracted.

On another occasion, she let me introduce learning logs into the class activities. This time I explained how we were to proceed with the log, what time would be allotted to write, what times I'd be reading through them, and so on. It was here that she interrupted and changed the plan on the spot, just after I had told the students how we were going to proceed. This, I felt, made me look foolish, and, in a way, I felt I lost some credibility with the students.

I eventually was given the freedom to choose what we were to study next in eighth-grade literature. I was excited about that. As it turned out, everything I chose, she opposed. Usually the last day before I would start a new lesson and after much preparation, she would approach me and say, "I have a better idea." It became very frustrating to say the least.

Now I don't know what to do to resolve the situation I'm in. Dr. Rugel expects that my lessons will be based on what I have learned in my education courses back at the college. I don't want to tell her what Ms. Collins has said about her or what she has said about whole language. At the same time, I don't want to cross Ms. Collins directly because that could make my stay at this school even worse. She can make it very miserable for me here. I am also quite aware that my letter of recommendation for a real teaching job will have to come from her. But how can I get the experience I need when Ms. Collins tries to control everything that happens?

Questions

1. Pretend that you are Ms. Collins. Write about this dilemma from her point of view. What, if anything, can you learn from considering her viewpoint?
2. What is the value of a whole language approach for teaching and learning?
3. Why, do you think, can disagreements arise about teaching methods espoused in education courses and methods currently used by teachers?
4. What are other issues in this case? Brainstorm a list and analyze possible courses of action.
5. How much control should student teachers have? Consider this in terms of classroom management, curriculum, daily scheduling, and so on.

CASE 60

The Conflict

Ross *Jussem, a student teacher in a large high school, has difficulties when a misunderstanding creates tension with one of his cooperating teachers. He struggles with how to patch things up and wonders how much this will affect his student teaching evaluation.*

Out of all the education classes I have taken, none of them prepared me for "the conflict." That's what I call the chain of events that led me to get caught in the middle of a dispute between two of the cooperating teachers at the large, urban high school where I carried out my student teaching.

I began the semester not knowing what to expect. I was excited as well as nervous, but this was what I had wanted to do all of my life, and now was my chance to do it. I was assigned to a team of three cooperating teachers: one for U.S. history, one for world history, and a third for a special topics course taken as an elective by seniors. I observed for two weeks and started teaching thereafter. I loved it!

The school was mostly Hispanic, with only 3 other male teachers compared to 63 female teachers. I was vaguely aware that two of my cooperating teachers, Ms. Vickers and Ms. Lynn, had had a long-standing dispute, but that had nothing to do with me, I reasoned. It seemed to me that I was accepted with open arms by the faculty and the students. I ate lunch every day with the teachers, and on my birthday, one of my cooperating teachers gave me a school sweatshirt. I felt like I was part of the family.

One of my cooperating teachers, Ms. Vickers, mentioned to the principal that I would like to teach in that school if there were any openings. He said that there were no positions at the time but informed me that I would be first on the list if one opened up. I was excited, to say the least. Ms. Vickers was really on my side and was pushing for me.

The trouble began only three days before Easter vacation, when I was suddenly informed I would be held responsible for prepping the eleventh graders who were soon to be taking the state standardized tests. I felt a lot of pressure as a student teacher but said, "No problem; I'll do it." Ms. Vickers said she thought it was unfair that I had this responsibility but that the principal had requested it. Like I said, I was very nervous, but I guessed this is what happens in the real world of teaching.

Easter came and went, and before I knew it, I was back in school. I noticed that Ms. Vickers seemed different. Two weeks went by, and I felt like something was wrong, but I had no idea what. Then it happened. I had forgotten to make some copies and was leaving the class, and Ms. Vickers asked me in an angry voice, "Where are you supposed to be right now?" I told her I had to make copies, but she gave me a lecture on being well prepared for class. Then she said what was really bothering her.

"I heard through the grapevine that you have been complaining about being held responsible for the state testing. I was told that you went to Ms. Lynn to complain."

I tried to tell her I had not complained. I had only mentioned the testing in passing, but Ms. Vickers was irate, "Well, I heard that you weren't happy about the situation."

From that day on, things have only gotten worse. I was hoping that Ms. Vickers would just drop the matter and we could move on, but no such luck. Only four weeks of student teaching are left, and she often ignores me, reprimands me for little things, and rarely even makes eye contact. What started out to be a great experience is turning into a nightmare.

If it weren't for Ms. Lynn, I don't know what I would do. She has made a point of being very supportive and told me not to worry about a thing. She confided to me that Ms. Vickers has been teaching for more than 20 years and feels that she has to be in charge of everything. While it is comforting to have someone who sympathizes, I worry about how the conflict with Ms. Vickers will affect my grade and if I still have a chance of getting a job in this school. What's more, I'm at a loss to know how I got into this bind in the first place. I wonder if it's possible to patch things up with Ms. Vickers and how I can go about doing it now.

Questions

1. Explain this case from the viewpoint of each of the three main characters. What can you learn? Does this give you a different outlook on the case?
2. How can student teachers avoid becoming involved in conflicts that arise in school settings? Should personal conflicts be expected in any job? To what degree are personal conflicts in a teaching job different from those in other settings?
3. How would you handle a conflict with your cooperating teacher or other school personnel? What advice would you give Ross?
4. What are some of the other issues that arise in this case? Brainstorm as many as you can.
5. Relate this case to Daniel Goleman's ideas about emotional intelligence. How important are social skills and emotional control in any job?

CASE 61

A Matter of Exhaustion

Jeffrey Voorhees, student teaching in high school math, wonders why no one told him how demanding student teaching would be. He worries that his failure to successfully juggle his responsibilities is affecting his relationship with his cooperating teacher and his teaching abilities.

I am in the seventh week of student teaching, and the pressure is really starting to mount. Between preparing for lessons, actual teaching, checking homework, preparing for college classes, working in a part-time job, seeing my girlfriend, and responding to family demands, I have absolutely no energy to devote to any one thing. The work is starting to pile up, and every night I get less and less sleep.

I woke up at 7:10 this morning as I usually do. This gives me just enough time to shower, get dressed, and still make it to school with not a minute to spare. "Why didn't anyone warn me about the total exhaustion I would feel?" I ask myself. "Seven more weeks and it will all be over. How will I ever be able to pull this off?"

I walked into the high school and mustered up enough energy to smile and say hello to my cooperating teacher and some of the students who were already in the classroom. Inside my head I thought, "I know I didn't prepare enough for the lesson I'll be teaching in 15 minutes. I know they're going to ask me questions that I don't have answers for." I had begun working on this particular math lesson at ten o'clock the preceding night, immediately after getting home from my night class at the college. By two in the morning, I had typed up all the handouts I would be distributing to the class, but I was too tired to reread the chapter in the text.

I managed to make it through the lesson, but when it was over, the frustration set in. "This could have been so much better if I could've had more time to work on it," I thought. It had been a long time since my cooperating teacher had said, "That was a fine lesson. It went really well." Ms. Chase has been so helpful and supportive that I feel great pressure not to let her down. I wanted to prove to her what a great teacher I can be, but it'll have to be on another day.

The following day was no different. With very little time to prepare, I hastily looked through the teacher's companion to the textbook and made 25 copies of a crossword puzzle relating to some of the math terms that the class is studying. Ms. Chase said nothing to me as the students worked on the puzzle. I imagined what she must be thinking. All the creative projects I told her about the first week; all the interesting approaches I wanted to try: she must be thinking that it was all just talk. Somehow I need to catch up. I need to impress her.

I called in sick at my job to work on lessons for the following day and to catch up on some other work around the house. After hours of brainstorming and research, I came up with a great lesson and spent another two hours refining it. "This is great. This is what I know I'm capable of," I thought to myself as I put everything away. I went to sleep content with what I had accomplished, and the fact that the household chores weren't done didn't even affect me.

The following day, I presented my lesson to my first-period class, and it went off beautifully. For the first time in weeks, I felt good about myself, and my feelings were reinforced by positive comments from the students. To top it off, my cooperating teacher approached me after class with a big smile and said, "That was excellent! I knew you had it in you."

During the break in the teachers' room, Ms. Chase and I sat together. She said to me, "It must have taken you a lot of time to put that lesson together, but I think it really paid off. The students loved it. I think the 10th and 11th graders would enjoy it, too. If you feel you're ready, you could present a version of this lesson to them. I know we had talked a while ago about your taking over more classes. I think you're ready for it." These are two classes I had sat in on for the past seven weeks but had done nothing more than observe. Seeing the confidence and enthusiasm in Ms. Chase's face, how could I say no?

"Sure, that sounds great," I said.

I got into my car after school and thought, "How will I find the energy to take on two more classes if I barely have enough time for the two I have now? How can I follow up what I did today?"

Questions

1. Is time the only issue in this case? Explain your answer.
2. Brainstorm a list of possible courses of action that Jeffrey might take to deal with the time constraints he is facing.
3. What adjustments in your own schedule are needed in order to maximize the benefits of your student teaching?
4. How do the time constraints of a student teacher compare to those of a regular classroom teacher?
5. How important is preparation in teaching? What personal examples can you give?

CASE 62

No Time to Be Both Teacher and Student

Patricia *Durant becomes convinced that the assignments required in her college seminar course in addition to her other responsibilities are detracting from her student teaching in a high school where she hopes to be hired.*

As I arrived for my first day of student teaching at Wilson High School, I was filled with anticipation and anxiety. Although I had been a substitute teacher in the district for two years, I realized that the time to prove myself had finally arrived. "The anxiety will eventually disperse," I thought as I approached the main office, ready to embark on my career as an educator. My familiarity with the school and the staff eased my tension, but the prospect of facilitating a class was daunting. I understood that teaching and learning was a process. At times, it may take an individual many years to become the outstanding educator that students deserve. I was up for the challenge!

As my cooperating teacher and I became more familiar with each other, we truly hit it off. We routinely met after school to talk about the past lessons and to discuss future ideas. Ms. Wilson and I sometimes even met on weekends to discuss the upcoming week's agenda. After the first month, I genuinely loved teaching, and I enjoyed working with my cooperating teacher. There was one problem, however. The amount of work required to teach appropriately was vast and extremely time-consuming. I did not mind the preparation and constraints placed on me by my cooperating teacher, but what did bother me was the seemingly meaningless work and assignments that my college professor gave me in the seminar we took along with our student teaching.

My conflict was intensified when I discovered that there would be a teaching position opening at the school where I was student teaching. In fact, a few staff members mentioned to me that if I continued to do a good job at the school, they could see no reason why I would not get hired. At this point, I really took the bull by the horns. I submerged myself into my student teaching experience and created lessons that my cooperating teacher deemed better than some taught by 10-year veterans. My total dedication yielded me many sleepless nights but much satisfaction. I really established a great rapport with my students, and my daily teaching was an event that brought a lot of laughter and fulfillment.

Each week seemed to be flying by, every day getting increasingly better, when, without warning, Thursday would arrive. Thursday was the day that I had to travel in order to attend the student teaching seminar. Now the seminar had been organized as a support group in which students could discuss their experiences during the week that had just passed, but it was also a typical college class with reflections on abstract educational theory and mandatory attendance. I felt that the heavy workload in the seminar was really unfair. After all I was responsible for three preps. There was no way that I could complete the weekly journal assignments given by my college professor and maintain a high standard in my student teaching. "Does he realize how much time it takes to prepare for three separate classes?" I routinely asked myself. "I barely have time to breathe." I was also affected by the exciting prospect of receiving a job at the high school. If I let down on my efforts to prepare thoroughly, I might jeopardize my status at the school and my future job possibility.

Dr. Tompkins, my professor at college, did not seem very sympathetic with my plight. He was adamant about his stance, and it seemed as though my pleas about compromising on workload were being uttered in vain. Could I afford to blow off my college work? I had really had enough of theory and reflection, and I wanted to immerse myself in the real world of teaching. If I didn't complete this work, though, there was a strong possibility that I might fail the class. Then I would have to repeat the entire class over again. But should I sacrifice some of my precious time and energy from teaching in order to complete successfully my college assignments? I felt that if I did this, my lessons would suffer, and I might not continue to enjoy a reputation as a hard worker in the high school. The potential for a chance-of-a-lifetime job was on the horizon. Where should my loyalties lie?

Questions

1. How important is educational theory once you get into the field? Explain your opinions.
2. Write a paragraph describing this situation from Dr. Tompkins's point of view. Why, do you think, does he feel that journal reflections are so important?
3. Has teaching, and especially preparing for class, been more time-consuming than you expected? What aspects of teaching have taken up the most time outside of class?
4. How much preparation should a teacher be expected to do outside of class time? Are the preparation periods given to teachers enough time? Discuss.
5. How should Patricia handle this dilemma? What choices does she have? How else could she gain more time for her work?

For Further Reading

Clark, C. (1995). *Thoughtful teaching.* New York: Teachers College Press.

This book speaks to teachers, teacher educators, students, and researchers in a deep, complex way. It considers thoughtful teaching, research on thoughtful teaching, portraits of thoughtful teaching, and cultivating thoughtful teaching. It also provides a mix of research, storytelling, interviews, and personal narrative that will make the reader think and feel differently about teaching.

Covey, S. (1989). *The 7 habits of highly effective people: Powerful lessons in personal change.* New York: Simon & Schuster.

This popular trade book presents an approach for solving personal and professional problems with step-by-step principles and insightful anecdotes.

Goleman, D. (1995). *Emotional intelligence: Why it can matter more than IQ.* New York: Bantam.

This volume looks at what it means to be smart, the nature of emotional intelligence, and how emotional intelligence applies to us as adults in our own lives and in our teaching.

Henry, E., Huntley, J., McKamey, C., & Harper, L. (1995). *To be a teacher: Voices from the classroom.* Thousand Oaks, CA: Corwin Press.

This compelling personal account of four new teachers at Mark Twain Middle School documents their struggles, values, beliefs, strengths and weaknesses, knowledge, and skills. It offers a realistic view of life in the classroom that new teachers will find affirming.

Louis, K. S., & Kruse, S. D. (1995). *Professionalism and community: Perspectives on reforming urban schools.* Thousand Oaks, CA: Corwin Press.

This book uses an analysis of various schools to present the structural, social, and human conditions of schooling and a framework for evaluating the elements of community. Appropriate for teachers, school leaders, and policy-makers, this book shows why so many well-intentioned, well-planned reforms fail, while offering important lessons and keys to making reform efforts work.

PART III
Reflecting on Teaching: Writing Your Own Case

You're in the field. Maybe you're carrying out your first observation or even embarking on the long-awaited chance to put all that you have learned so far into practice in an actual classroom. In either case, you are undoubtedly experiencing the exhilarating yet disconcerting whirlwind of demands that envelop beginning teachers. Classrooms can be confusing places, and practitioners often must think and act quickly. The cases in this book were designed to sharpen your perceptions and give you strategies to approach the dilemmas that arise in school settings. But no two experiences are exactly the same. While examining dilemmas posed by other practitioners can provide you with a repertoire of virtual experience upon which to draw in rethinking your own teaching, writing your own case based on your unique classroom situation is also a valuable learning experience.

In our college classes, we begin the semester by reading and analyzing various published teaching cases. During this time, we encourage our students to continually think of issues and concerns that could be developed into their own teaching cases. Our students write a first draft of their cases about halfway through the semester and then bring them to class to share with their peers. Using the feedback they receive, the students edit their cases and in a few weeks hand in their finished versions. As many as possible of these cases are shared in small groups or with the whole class and analyzed in the same way in which we use the published cases.

Why Write Your Own Teaching Case?

Writing your own student teaching case can help you become more reflective in your own teaching by learning to *problem pose*: that is, to identify and critically look at hidden or not-so-hidden obstacles to effective teaching. When we write, we do not merely report events as they occurred in the past; rather, we *reconstruct* those events, considering them from new perspectives. Writing is a form of thinking in which the writer constantly sifts through experiences, making choices, connections, and even revisions in beliefs. Writing a case can help you change your approaches to real situations in your teaching. By rethinking your actions, you can go beyond merely reacting to predicaments you face in the classroom and instead make teaching a more conscious activity. The process of writing helps you to generate ideas and to explore alternatives. Your case presents an opportunity to span the gap between theory and practice.

An additional advantage of reflecting through writing is that you can gain necessary distance from classroom dilemmas, making it easier to determine what steps to take. Just reading your own words on paper can help you see alternatives that otherwise might not have occurred to you. You can use the case to observe yourself and your practice in the same way that you would carry out an observation of another teacher or perhaps watch a video of your teaching.

Your own teaching case can also provide the basis for helpful discussion and feedback from your peers, who form one of the most empathic audiences for your thoughts about teaching and learning. Because a teaching case simply presents dilemmas instead of giving answers, your peers may more readily feel invited to join with you in problem-solving.

Learning to See

One of the most difficult tasks in writing a teaching case is learning to look closely at what is happening in the classroom. Whether you are student teaching or observing classrooms, you will sometimes find it necessary to step out of the hectic pace of the classroom environment to learn how to view a phenomenon in-depth. Often prospective teachers focus solely on what the teacher is doing and may miss the signs emanating from the learners themselves that indicate what learning is truly taking place. Body language, interactions among students, acting out, daydreaming, repeatedly going to the bathroom, fiddling with pencils and erasers—all can provide valuable clues about teaching issues.

Because the classroom is such a busy place, it may be important to practice the act of seeing. By looking at a familiar place such as your school cafeteria and trying to see it in an unfamiliar way, you may become more aware of the hidden dynamics there. Just looking consciously can help you become aware of the cafeteria workers, whose presence is sometimes taken so much for granted that they become nearly invisible. Such an activity can help you get beyond things that most of us take for granted in schools and really question what is going on and whether it is helpful for learners.

ACTIVITY 1

Learning to See

A practice observation of a familiar place can help you learn how to look at your own classroom. Begin by brainstorming a list of places on your campus, such as the student center, the cafeteria, the library, and other familiar gathering places. Break into groups of three. Each group will select one place on campus to observe carefully for 10 minutes. As you observe your site, try to view it with fresh eyes as though you are seeing it for the first time. Note particulars about the setting, the people present, what is going on. Is anything unusual taking place?

It is important that you not speak to other members of your group about what you have seen. After you return to the class, free-write for 10 minutes, making a log of your observations. Write in as much detail as possible. After 10 minutes, have your group members take turns reading aloud their logs. As each group member reads, observe what is different from and what is similar to what you have seen. Discuss possible reasons for the differences between your log and those of the other two observers. Do not feel too bad if you did not see all that your peers saw. Any site, but especially a classroom, has so much activity that it is impossible to see everything. Also, no two people see through exactly the same lens. We all filter what we observe through our own experiences and perspectives.

Next, look closely at your group's observations for implications concerning gender, race, class, sexuality, or other issues. If these issues did not come up in the logs, discuss what you saw and ask if any of these issues arose out of your observation. Social issues are difficult to perceive in any situation. Consciously trying to tease out these issues can help you be more aware in your own teaching.

What to Write About

Most beginning teachers find that they have an abundance of topics for their cases. For many, the real problem involves trying to decide which topic to write about. If you find yourself brimming with so many questions that you don't know which one to focus on, don't be reluctant to consider several of them. Try them all on for size. Is this a case that goes to the heart of your efforts to develop as a teacher? What might you learn by pursuing this case? After reflecting in-depth on a few of your ideas, ask yourself: Which is the most compelling issue? What do you genuinely want to know how to handle?

Several learners in our classes have voluntarily written more than one case because of their desire to use writing to explore a number of issues that they felt passionate about. A few student teachers, however, initially say that they have nothing to write about. A beginning teacher may worry, for example, that writing a student teaching case might lead to criticizing his or her cooperating teacher or other authority figures. Most cases aren't that simple and have more to do with exploring choices *you* need to make rather than focusing solely on the way others act. There is a difference between criticism of others and an examination of your relationships with others. Whatever your situation may be, try to remember that this is *your* case. Any dilemma you are genuinely facing—whether because of your relationship with your cooperating teacher, with your supervisor, with the faculty at your school, with the students, or with other student teachers—can be explored honestly and openly. That is why you must always use pseudonyms and otherwise disguise the school in which you are teaching.

Sometimes student teachers blessed with strong cooperating teachers in progressive and supportive settings also may believe that there is little to write about since classroom life appears to proceed with few overt difficulties. Just because things go smoothly, however, does not mean that there are no problems. You might, for example, study students who do not talk much or who are excessively well behaved. What is going on with them? Are they learning? How might you enable them to develop confidence and skills in speaking and to assert their needs as learners?

Another way to bring hidden dilemmas to the surface is to ask yourself what you find yourself talking about with other student teachers. You may be surprised at what you learn through reflecting on your conversations with peers who are going through similar experiences. One of the authors of a case in this book got her idea from a friend who noticed that the student teacher often talked about her difficulties in balancing the diametrically opposed educational philosophies of her supervisor and her cooperating teacher. Opportunities for such in-depth discussions can be incorporated into a student teaching or observation seminar (see Activity 2), or you might simply reflect on your own interactions with other beginning teachers.

Another way to uncover topics for cases is to keep an ongoing journal. Your journal provides you with a personal place in which you don't have to be consistent, justify your ideas to anyone else, or worry about the formal aspects of writing. Instead, you can enjoy the freedom of focusing on an honest dialogue with yourself in which you explore contradictions and alternative perspectives concerning your internship.

ACTIVITY 2

Gathering Ideas from Peers

Small-group forums can help you to find your topic. Break into groups of five. Choose a timekeeper and a note taker for a report back to the class as a whole. Let each group member identify a dilemma that he or she is facing as a student teacher and answer questions and hear comments about the dilemma from other group members. Those who are having trouble finding a topic can seek help from the group. Give each person 10 minutes. Then report to the class as a whole about the dilemmas that your group members are facing. Hearing about other student teachers' situations also may help you identify a topic for your own student teaching case.

Beginning to Write

Case writing differs from other academic writing in that it is less abstract, can be in the first person, and more openly tells a story. Ironically, despite its focus on a real-life situation, a case shares many similarities with fiction. Like a work of fiction, a case must have a strong opening, a setting, and developed, believable characters, who, like people in real life, are neither all good nor all bad but complex and human. Also like fiction, a case is based around a conflict that progresses to a climax in which the characters are confronted with choices. Unlike fiction, however, there is no resolution of the conflict. The resolution is left open for readers to construct.

The first paragraph of your case can introduce the main characters, describe the setting, and include a summary of the dilemma that the student teacher is facing. As we noted earlier, you need to make up pseudonyms for yourself, all the characters in your case, and the school setting. Some case writers also disguise the city or town in which the case takes place. Assigning pseudonyms is an important protection for you and the school you are writing about. The pseudonyms should be used even in class discussions about your case.

Like a fiction writer, you want your case to come alive. Do not be reluctant to place yourself solidly in the case and let your readers know your hopes, your fears, and your reactions to what is going on. Unlike most fiction, teaching cases have authors who are also characters in the narrative. You want your readers to identify with you, to see as you see, to experience your conflicts. While some case authors prefer to use the third person as a way of getting some distance from their stories, others find the first-person vantage point to be most effective in allowing readers to vicariously experience the dilemma being presented.

In addition to a description of the physical appearance and personal habits of you and the other main characters, you can describe in vivid detail the context in which the case occurs. What does the classroom look like? Sound like? Smell like? Is the school on a busy street? What kind of neighborhood or city is the school in? Such heavy description will invite your readers to imagine themselves in your story and thereby become more involved in considering possible resolutions to your case.

Your beginning may state or indicate the dilemma that you face. This way your reader won't be wondering where the case is leading but can look for clues about possible resolutions while reading. For example, you as a reader would no doubt be much more interested in a case that states up front, "What is a student teacher to do when she suspects a child is being abused at home?" rather than one in which you have to wait halfway through the case to find out what is at issue. Of course, writing styles vary, and some authors prefer to dramatically lead up to the main conflict.

Your first sentence will decide whether a reader will continue reading your case. Think of the beginning as advertising for your writing. To make it snappy and enticing, you might ask a provocative question, make a controversial statement, use an in-depth description of the setting, or incorporate an interesting quotation from one of your main characters. You can use your creativity in deciding how to induce readers to take your case seriously, to experience what you have experienced, and to help you choose courses of action.

If, after reading all this, you still have trouble committing that first word to paper, you can use several techniques to break through blocks. One valuable technique is called free-writing (see Activity 3). You can do this with your classmates or by yourself. The purpose of free-writing is to make contact with your inner voice, that part of you that carries out constant dialogue through what we call thinking. All of us have a steady stream of words to draw on, but sometimes we are so critical of our own efforts that we interrupt the flow of our thoughts so that the words come out disjointed if at all.

ACTIVITY 3

Free-Writing

Free-writing, a common technique used in many composition classes, can help you actually get started. First, get out a pen and paper. Take 10 minutes and write steadily. Write down everything that comes into your mind; don't even lift your pen off the page. If you are stuck, you can write the word *stuck* over and over again, or you can repeat the last word that you wrote until a new idea pops into your head. Try not to criticize yourself. Free-writing is supposed to sound like a jumble. After you have spent 10 minutes writing, reread what you have written, underlining any ideas that you may want to develop further. You may be surprised at what you discover.

And Now the Rest of the Story

Once you have begun your student teaching case, introduced your characters and setting, and delineated the dilemma, you are on the road toward a finished case. You need simply to tell the rest of the story and then leave the reader hanging at the end. The problem that you are describing should contain all the contradictions that pop up in everyday life. The case should be like life itself, in which issues are not all one-sided and solutions to problems are not obvious.

Some writers, especially those used to writing fiction, have a difficult time leaving a case hanging without resolving the conflict. While it may be tempting to include hints about possible solutions, especially when you're worried about how your readers might judge you, it is extremely important to *problem pose* at the end of your case. This means summarizing again the dilemma that the student teacher is facing so that your reader can ponder it.

Now you're finished! You've completed your case. To present the strongest case possible, however, revision can be very helpful. If you break the word *revision* into two parts—*re-vision*—you can see that it means re-seeing, reflecting on your case through other lenses, from other perspectives. This can be a rewarding activity for you, especially if carried out in groups in a college classroom (see Activity 4). Yet even if you are working on your case alone, you must go back and rework what you have written. Each time you do so, you may clarify what is bothering you and learn something new about your student teaching situation.

Activity 4

Revision: A New View

Revision can make your student teaching case a powerful learning tool for you and your readers. To work collaboratively on revision, bring three copies of your student teaching case to class. Break into groups of three. Give a copy of your case to each of your group members. Focus on each person's case for 20 or 30 minutes (depending on the length of your class period). When it is your turn, first read your case aloud. Then listen as the group members respond orally. Next, let them take a few minutes to respond in writing on their copy of the case. Decide which of them will respond to the content of your case and which will pay special attention to its form. (See "Guidelines for Responding to Peer Writing" at the end of this section.) Repeat this process each until group member has received feedback from the other two.

Using Cases to Problem-Solve

Once you have satisfactorily revised your case, you are ready to formally discuss it in class. Depending on class size, your professors may prefer that student teaching cases be shared in small groups. Small groups can be a safe place to explore opinions frankly and can furnish a place in which to get intensive feedback from a few classmates. Opportunities for in-depth feedback are fewer in large-group settings, but case writers have the advantage of hearing from more people, thereby seeing their dilemma from a wider range of viewpoints. Also, the class itself can encounter more situations that can arise during the student teaching period and benefit from discussing a greater variety of problems. In our own classes, we have used both small- and large-group sessions to maximize problem-solving (see Activity 5).

ACTIVITY 5

Group Problem-Solving

Small groups can be used to maximize reflection on your student teaching case. Bring four copies of your completed case to class. After the class breaks into small groups of four people each, distribute your writing to your other three group members. Choose a timekeeper, a group facilitator, and two people to report back to the large group. Let person read his or her case while the others silently follow along. Then spend 15 minutes discussing and providing feedback concerning the dilemma raised. The responders should try to connect the learning theories they have studied in their teacher education program to the cases that are being analyzed. For example, if the case involves difficulties that the student teacher is having with using small groups, they might want to consider readings they may have done on cooperative learning. After an hour, prepare to give a five-minute report to the entire class on the issues raised by the cases in your group and the possible resolutions it has considered.

Large-group feedback can also help you problem-solve with your student teaching case and provide you with feedback from a wider range of your peers. This activity can take one to three class periods, depending on the length of your class. To begin, the whole class arranges their chairs in a large circle. Your instructor or a student volunteer can serve as timekeeper. Pads of Post-it® notes to use for feedback will be distributed to the entire group. Each student will read aloud his or her case. Then the group members will each take two minutes to write feedback on a Post-it,® which will be passed to the author of the case at the end of two minutes.

When you are giving feedback, focus on solutions to the problem raised. Try to be as concrete as possible. For example, if the case involves the student teacher's efforts to get class members to break out of ethnically based cliques, as one of the cases in this book does, you might know of a get-acquainted activity that promotes respect for others' cultures. By all means, use this occasion to communicate any positive suggestions that can help the case author.

After you have read your case to the group, you will receive 25 or so Post-it® notes. Take these home, make a list of all of the suggestions, and write a reflection on their relative merits as well as on any ideas that may have occurred to you after reading your case and considering your classmates' responses.

Box 1

Guidelines for Writing a Student Teaching Case

1. Pay close attention to what is happening to you as a student teacher. Try not to take anything for granted but question everything, asking yourself, "What are the real problems I'm having?"

2. Look for key incidents and teachable moments in your practice when you're posed with a decision about something and honestly don't know what to do.

3. Consider issues you find yourself discussing with other student teachers outside your classes. This is a valuable way to tap into the real issues. Remember, this case is designed to help you. No pedagogical issues are taboo. Everyone faces problems in his or her teaching; to honestly look at your own problems is a sign of strength, not weakness, and is a precondition for growth.

4. Jot down notes during the day when you notice that something is bothering you. These notes can be a rich source of material for developing cases. You may want to put these into a journal to reflect on later.

5. Try to avoid focusing solely on a problem student or someone who you think should be referred. Instead look at your problems as a student

teacher. The case should concern a topic that you wished someone had discussed with you before you began your internship.

6. In order for your case to provide a basis for rich discussion from multiple points of view, the real event that you use should imply no easy or obvious answer. Teaching cases, like life itself, usually involve gray areas in which there is no one right or wrong way.

7. Once you have selected your topic, provide a full description of the setting and the principal characters involved.

8. Use pseudonyms for all students, teachers, and others to whom you refer and make up a name for the school and its location. Disguising your case in this way is an important protection for you and all concerned.

9. Be creative! While there is no canned format for writing a teaching case, your case will be strengthened by having a strong, snappy opening that clearly states the dilemma. You may want to begin with a quotation, a question, or an unusual situation that will draw readers in.

10. The emphasis in these cases is on what the student teacher—not the cooperating teacher or the students themselves—should do. You won't resolve your teaching problems by concentrating on what others should be doing.

11. Good cases end with a dilemma that the student teacher will need to solve. Contrary to most stories, in which resolution of the conflict usually occurs near the conclusion, the teaching case remains unresolved, demanding that its reader tie up the loose ends in imaginative ways. You may wish to end the case by summarizing the alternatives that the student teacher faces in solving the dilemma.

12. Reflect on your case as it is in the process of being written. Test out the first draft with other student teachers. Did the case generate interest? Is it complex enough? Are there areas of confusion? Does it lead to full discussion? Go back and complete the case based on your own insights and the reactions and suggestions of your readers.

Box 2

Guidelines for Responding to Peer Writing

1. Try to focus on positive feedback. What are the strengths of the writing?

2. Empty praise does not help anyone. Make sure that you believe what you say.

3. Be specific. For example, instead of responding, "This was interesting," or "You write well," you might say, "I think that the dilemma you presented in

your case would lead to much discussion among student teachers, because . . . " Then go on to list concrete reasons.

4. Try to avoid value judgments. The purpose of your response is to enable the writer to understand how someone is reading his or her text.

5. Try not to rehash what others have written. If you can bring a fresh perspective, however, by all means do so. Also, if you don't agree with other responses, feel free to state another opinion or an alternative reading of the text.

6. Look for clarity. If something is unclear to you, ask questions of the writer or restate what you understand the author to be writing.

7. Are there ways in which the case writer can more fully develop the case? Do you have concrete, positive suggestions that might help the writer?

8. Do you find the descriptions vivid? Can you picture the setting? You may want to share with the author your view of the setting or ask questions that might lead him or her to go into greater detail.

9. Is the resolution too obvious to you? Do you have suggestions that might make the case more multidimensional?

10. Do you find the characters believable? In cases, as in real life, there are usually no good guys or bad guys, only real teachers, real student teachers, and real students in situations that can be both difficult and exhilarating.

11. Have fun! Responding to writing, whether that of peers or of our students, can be both enjoyable and educational. Let's use these responses to have a dialogue about ideas.

For Further Reading

Barnes, L. B., Christensen, C., & Hansen, A. (Eds.). (1994). *Teaching and the case method: Text, cases, and readings* (3rd ed.). Boston: Harvard Business School Press.

This case book, developed at Harvard University's School of Business, pioneered the use of the case method in teaching. The authors discuss what a case is, how cases are used, how to gather data, and how to write cases.

Bogdan, R., & Biklen, S. (1982). *Qualitative research for education: An introduction to theory and methods.* Boston: Allyn & Bacon.

This classic work includes a history of qualitative research as well as how-to sections on carrying out observations, keeping field logs, interpreting data, and writing.

Coles, W. E., Jr., & Vopat, J. (Eds.). (1985). *What makes writing good: A multiperspective.* Lexington, MA: Heath.

Writing teachers such as Wayne Booth, Toby Fulwiler, Andrea Lunsford, Donald Murray, and Ira Shor analyze student texts and reflect on what constitutes good writing.

Elbow, P. (1973). *Writing without teachers.* New York: Oxford University Press.

This classic details steps in the writing process, with sections on free writing, peer response, and revision. A special feature explains Elbow's concept of playing the "believing" and "doubting" games as a way of achieving a fuller understanding of any subject.

Mayher, J. (1990). *Uncommon sense: Theoretical practice in language education.* Portsmouth, NH: Boynton/Cook.

This book calls for an "uncommonsense" approach to language learning that requires shedding taken-for-granted notions and engaging in critical reflection. Of interest is a section on uncommonsense writing competence, which stresses the recursive rather than the linear nature of the writing process.

Mayher, J., Lester, B., & Pradl, G. (1983). *Learning to write/writing to learn.* Upper Montclair, NJ: Boynton/Cook.

The authors emphasize that writing is an important tool for learning. Especially relevant are chapters on constructing the world through writing, the composing process, and responses to and evaluations of writing.

Pradl, G. (Ed.). (1982). *Prospect and retrospect: Selected essays of James Britton.* Upper Montclair, NJ: Boynton/Cook.

This collection by English educator James Britton includes essays on writing as a tool for exploring and reflecting on meaning. Included is a chapter discussing Britton's theory of participant and spectator roles in writing.

Rosenblatt, L. (1978). *The reader, the text, the poem: The transactional theory of the literary work.* Carbondale IL: Southern Illinois University Press.

The author shows that in any reading of a written work there is a transaction between the reader and the text whereby the reader constructs meaning based on what has been read.